DEDICATION

"This book is dedicated with deep respect and gratitude to the scholars whose passion for understanding the rich tapestry of Hindu culture has illuminated our paths. To Ananda Coomaraswamy, whose insightful interpretations have been a guiding light; Sir John Woodroffe (Arthur Avalon), whose explorations into Indian culture have opened new horizons; Sister Nivedita, whose eloquent writings have touched our hearts; C.F. Oldham, for his diligent exploration into the lore of serpents and their cultural significance; and J. Ph. Vogel, whose work in Indian archaeology and art history has enriched our understanding of the past. Your pioneering spirits have inspired this journey, and it is in the shadow of your scholarly dedication that this work humbly treads."

SACRED SERPENT

THE ANCIENT NAGA IN HINDU MYTHOLOGY

AJ CARMICHAEL

ACKNOWLEDGMENTS

First and foremost, I extend my heartfelt gratitude to the History Department of Banaras Hindu University (BHU). The faculty's profound knowledge and insightful perspectives on Hindu traditions and culture have been indispensable.

I am also profoundly thankful to the University of Delhi's Department of History. Their rigorous academic environment and encouragement of interdisciplinary research have significantly shaped the contours of this book. The stimulating discussions and debates held within their historic walls have greatly enriched my understanding and interpretation of Hindu spirituality and symbolism.

A special word of thanks is reserved for Dr. Aarav Krishnamurthy, a scholar whose name may not be widely recognized but whose contributions to the field of Hindu studies are monumental. Dr. Krishnamurthy, with his deep-rooted knowledge of ancient Hindu texts and traditions, provided critical insights, particularly in interpreting the Naga's role and symbolism in various historical contexts. His unique perspective and unwavering support have been a guiding light throughout the journey of writing this book.

To all the unnamed scholars, students, and enthusiasts of Hindu culture and history who have shared their thoughts and feedback, I am deeply thankful. Your passion for understanding and preserving the richness of Hindu spirituality has been a constant source of inspiration.

Lastly, I acknowledge the support of my family and friends, who have been my pillars of strength and patience throughout the demanding process of bringing this book to fruition. This work is as much a product of your belief in me as it is of my dedication to the subject.

Thank you all for being part of this enlightening journey.

INTRODUCTION

This book frequently returns to the theme of duality, particularly in relation to the serpent and the sun. In addition to signifying danger, dishonesty, and death, the serpent also symbolizes rebirth, transformation, and healing. In a similar vein, the sun represents both harshness and destruction in addition to life, energy, and growth. The investigation of this duality implies that knowledge of these two facets is necessary to comprehend both the natural world and the human predicament. The distinction between mythology and historical truth is becoming increasingly hazy, demonstrating how actual occurrences and cultures have shaped myths and legends and how those have, in turn, influenced them. It is argued that myths are more than just fantastic stories; rather, they have deep roots in societal advancements and human experiences. This emphasizes how crucial mythology is to how we perceive the world and ourselves.

The book explores the symbolic meanings of the sun and serpent in psychology. Based on Carl Jung's theories of archetypes and the collective unconscious it clarifies why these symbols are so universally recognizable and appealing. The symbols are believed to resonate with deeply ingrained psychological concepts and experiences that everyone shares, making them useful tools for reflection and understanding of behavior in others. Numerous studies conducted in a range of cultural contexts highlight the idea that human belief systems are both universal and diverse. The book provides examples of how various societies have integrated and understood the symbols of the sun and the serpent in ways that are particular to their own historical settings and cultural norms. This demonstrates the diversity of human expression in culture and the interdependence of human societies.

It highlights how these symbols have evolved and how they have endured over time. The study looks at how the sun and the serpent have changed over time, adjusting to new social, religious, and cultural norms while maintaining their fundamental symbolic meanings. This theme captures the fluidity of human beliefs and the ongoing conversation that shapes symbols and meanings between the past and present. When taken as a whole, these themes provide a thorough grasp of the breadth and complexity of the investigation into the symbolism of the sun and serpent. A character analysis or a commentary on the writing style and approach employed in the book may come next. An interdisciplinary approach is used in the work, combining psychology, anthropology, history, and mythology. This method enables a nuanced interpretation of the ancient Naga serpent race meaning. To provide a more comprehensive understanding of these symbols, the book draws from a multitude of sources and traditions rather than restricting itself to a single cultural or historical perspective.

The style's comparative examination of sun and serpent symbolism in various cultures is an important component. The book provides insights into the similarities and differences in human thought and belief systems by carefully contrasting and comparing how different civilizations have interpreted and used these symbols. Historical facts are skillfully woven into mythological tales. The narrative style is captivating as it narrates a variety of myths and legends from around the globe, skillfully tying them in with historical occurrences and customs. This method of telling stories not only increases the book's readability but also demonstrates how ubiquitous these symbols have been throughout human history.

Mythology and their theories are often cited to explore the deeper meanings of the symbolism of the serpent. By drawing on common themes and archetypes, the book investigates the relationship between these symbols and the human psyche. This analysis gains depth from the psychological lens, which implies that these myths and symbols represent essential facets of human experience. The book is accessible to a wider audience despite its scholarly approach. Since arguments are well-supported by data and refrain from using unduly technical language, both scholars and general readers with an interest in mythology and symbolism will find the book to be interesting. The book does more than provide facts; it also offers a critical analysis and contemplation of the meanings associated with the snake and sun symbols. The significance of the work transcends historical and cultural boundaries, as readers are prompted to consider the influence of these symbols on modern culture and personal awareness.

The book explores these symbols' cultural and historical significance as well as their applicability in today's world. The serpent is still used in modern religious, cultural, and even business symbolism, with meanings of wisdom, healing, and rejuvenation. Like this, the sun continues to be a common icon in many contemporary forms of expression, from national flags and emblems to art and literature, representing life, energy, and authority. In the modern world, the debate over the psychological ramifications of these symbols is especially pertinent. In an age when the study of universal symbols such as the sun and the serpent is gaining popularity, it provides insightful information about the human psyche. These symbols, which have their roots in the collective unconscious, still have an impact on our goals, anxieties, and beliefs.

The book's examination of serpents' natural symbolism speaks to current worries about environmental preservation and our connection to the natural world. Many cultures' reverence or fear of snakes reflects their broader attitudes toward nature, emphasizing the need for harmony and respect in our relationships with the natural world. As a representation of life-giving energy, the sun also serves as a reminder of the value of sustainable practices and our reliance on natural resources. The book's multidisciplinary approach is one of its strongest points. A deep and complex understanding of the symbolism of the sun and serpent is possible when connections can be made between different academic disciplines. Comparative analysis works especially well to show how these symbols are diverse and universal across eras and cultures.

However, because psychology primarily sees these ancient mythological traditions through a Western psychological lens, it may restrict how these narratives are interpreted. Perspectives from various psychological theories or native interpretations of these symbols could be included in future research. Furthermore, even though a wide range of cultures are covered in detail, some regions or lesser-known customs may need to be adequately represented. All things considered; the book delves deeply into the analysis of two of the most enduring symbols in human history. Its synthesis of mythology, psychology, history, and cultural analysis provides a thorough understanding of the significance of the serpent and the sun. The book is still a useful tool for comprehending the profound ancient serpent worship ingrained in human consciousness and culture despite certain shortcomings. I have also provided detailed background subject matter as a powerful aid for the newcomers to this subject matter, particularly on Nagas and Hinduism.

Sculpture Cobra used for worship in South India.

1. THE HOODED SERPENT

The hooded serpent, also known as the Naga, Nag, or Cobra, is still highly revered in India, as it was once in many other countries. It is called the "good snake" and is regarded as a protector and omen of success. Even though the snake's poison is extremely lethal, very few Hindus can hurt a Naga, and even fewer are able to kill one. Living cobras were, and probably still are, brought in from the countryside for trade during the Nagapanchami festival, which is observed in many towns in honor of the serpent demigods. The locals bought these and released them from captivity as a deed of religious merit. Almost all large trees in India have a crudely carved picture of a serpent or, in its place, a round stone underneath them. Offerings made to these "Nags," as they are known, are safer for human consumption than snake food. Furthermore, lit candles and flowers are frequently placed in front of the shrines.

It is not necessary to believe that snakes are revered in all cultures. The Nag is holy in and of itself. It has been suggested that the aboriginal tribes were not the source of this serpent's reverence; rather, it is closely related to the worship of the sun in the orthodox Hindu religion. As we shall see later, the hooded serpent represented those who claimed to be descendants of the sun. Known in Brahmanical writings as "the celestial serpents belonging to Surya" (the sun god), the Naga demigods are the deified leaders of the solar race. These gods belong to a non-orthodox but popular class of deities that are still practiced in northern and southern India, with temples, priests, and devotees. Hindus first turn to these ancient deities, not the great gods of the Brahmans when things are bad. They make their vows to the Naga, also called the Deva, and ask them for rain to aid their crops during times of famine or pestilence. They also give them their cow's milk and the first fruits of their harvest.

According to the Mahabharata, Devas, Nagas, and a few other lesser gods were the residents of Swarga, the heaven that Indra ruled. European writers have traditionally referred to the Devas and the Nagas as gods, even though it is more accurate to refer to them as demigods. They were elevated mortals. It is essential to distinguish between the Naga demigods in heaven and the Naga people on Earth. The former were the deified ancestors of the latter. Although the Nagas are not specifically mentioned in the Veda, serpents are frequently mentioned in connection with Asuras or Dasyus and are described as Indra's and the Devas' enemies. According to Sayana's commentary, several eminent scholars have construed the Asuras, Dasyus, or Serpas of the Veda as atmospheric phenomena. These are Indra's adversaries in the eyes of the Brahmans, who see them as demons and usually represent them as humanoid monsters with animal heads. I wish to demonstrate how the Brahmans' Asuras or demons, the Asuras and Serpas of the Rig Veda, and the Asuras and Nagas of Manu and the Mahabharata were all representatives of the opposing tribes that resisted the Aryan invasion. As we shall see later, the Devas and the Nagas, or serpent gods, are still considered deified heroes.

In the Rig Veda, the Asuras or Dasyus are called Ahi, or serpents. In a hymn, for instance, "With his vast, destroying thunderbolt, Indra struck the darkling, mutilated Vritra; as the trunks of trees were felled by the axe, so lies Ahi prostrate on the earth." In addition, it is written: "The waters that delight the minds (of men) flow over him, recumbent on the earth, as a river burst through its broken banks; Ahi has been prostrated beneath the feet of the waters, which Vritra by his might had obstructed." A different hymn begins, "When thou, Indra, was inspirited by drinking the effused (Soma), the strong heaven was rent asunder with fear at the clamor of that Ahi; and thy thunderbolt, in its vigor, struck off the head of Vritra, the obstructor of heaven and earth." In all these passages, Ahi, the serpent, is identified with Vritra, who is mentioned in the Veda as one of the most powerful enemies of Indra and the Devas. Other hymns identify Aryas or the Devas as Ahi's adversaries; Tims states: "To that Indra, the women, the wives of the Devas, addressed their hymns on the destruction of Ahi."

The women mentioned in this passage are obviously the wives of the earthly Devas, or Aryas, not the wives of the gods. In an additional hymn, we read: "Mighty wielder of the thunderbolt, when the priests had thus exalted thee (by praise) and the exhilarating Soma juice had been drunk, thou did expect Ahi from the earth, manifesting thine own sovereignty." Following that, we have: "Indra, you did perform. a magnificent act, when thou used thy thunderbolt to awaken the dozing, Ahi." Arbuda was also a serpent, and other hymns state that "Thou, Indra, hast defended Kutsa in a fatal fight with Sushna; thou hast destroyed Sambara in defense of Atithigva; thou hast trodden with thy foot upon the great Arbuda." You were made in the beginning to vanquish oppressors." In his remarks in this passage, the commentator Sayana asserts that Kutsa was a rishi and that Sushna, Sambara, and Arbuda were Asuras. Other hymns refer to Arbuda as well, in which he is associated with both Dasyus and the Asuras. For instance, one hymn claims that Arbuda was "invigorated by (the libation of) the exulting Trita, offering thee the Soma, thou hast annihilated Arbuda." Priests propitiate, by the offering of the Soma, that Indra who slew Urana, displaying ninety-nine arms, and hurled Arbuda clown headlong."

In addition, we find out: "Thou hast extirpated Vritra with thy mighty weapons; thou hast been the destroyer of the deceptive Arbuda and Mrigaya; thou hast extricated the cattle from the mountain." Not only that but by eating the Soma, Indra was able to confuse the crafty Danava's devices. "When Indra, the friend of man, attempted to slay the enemy of humanity, the showerer's thunderbolts roared loudly." You can set the Dasyu aside with your left hand. Another passage says, "Hero Indra, maintain the strength with which thou hast crushed Vritra, the son of Danu, who resembles a spider, and let the Arya see the light." According to what we know, Vritra was an Asura, a Dasyu, a Danava, and so on; these were just different names for the same chief or people, and she belonged to the serpent race of Ahi.

Further proof that the Asuras, Dasyus, Daityas, and Danavas were hostile tribes can be found in the Sama Veda, where it is said that "all the gods, thy friends, deserted thee, Indra when fleeing from Vritra Asura's wrath" and "Indra, like a friend, advanced to the front of the battle and slew Vritra." Then we have: "All the moving tribes of men bow down before the wrath of Indra, as all the rivers bend toward the sea." He, like a hero, hewed down the hosts of the Danavas and, as a protector, subdued our foes." And further: "Indra is the devourer of Vritra, the overthrow of Bala, the destroyer of cities, and the shedder of water." He strikes off the head of the earth-shaking Vritra with his rain-causing, hundred-spiked vajra (thunderbolt). In each of these sections, Vritra appears as an Asura warrior. Vritra is also associated with the Atharva Veda, Asuras and Dasyus. As we can see, "With this talisman, Indra slew Vritra; with it, he, full of devices, destroyed the Asuras."

So, the Vedas give us ample evidence that the tribes that opposed Indra and the Aryas were serpentine, including the Asuras, Dasyus, Daityas, and Danavas. The authorities dispute these people's identities and places of origin. Let's attempt to ascertain. The events described in the Rig Vedic hymns most likely happened over a long period, starting before the Aryas came to India. As Haug has shown, the word "Asura" is synonymous with the Iranian "Ahura," and this title is used in some of the older Vedic hymns as an homage to Indra and other benevolent deities. However, the Asuras are defined very differently in later passages; the Devas used the term Asura, or its equivalent, to refer to enemies in general after the Devas and Asuras split up, much as Deva, or Daeva, became a pejorative term in Iran. These people were enemies of the Devas and the Asuras from the start, even before these two branches of the Aryan family broke apart. The Vendidad claims that the Azi-Dhaka who killed Yima and overthrew him is not entirely true, but both surely belonged to the same race, as did probably "the horse-devouring, man-devouring, serpent Sruara," whom the Iranian hero Keresaspa killed later. Angra Mainyu's creation, a formidable serpent, appeared, which was another factor in the exodus from Airyana Vaejo.

Later, the nickname "Azi-Dhaka" (the devouring serpent) was ascribed to a succession of kings. This dynasty is said to have started with Bevarasp and ended a millennium later. This king has been compared to Astyages, who was deposed by Feridun and sentenced to be shackled to the mountain of Demavand, according to Herodotus. According to legend, Feridun overthrew this king. Cyrus Astyages was the same as Istuvegu, who was supposedly defeated by Cyrus and Babylonian King Nabonidus at Ekbatana, or Agamtanu. The relationship between Azi-Dhaka and Istuvegu is currently unknown. The narrative about the latter found in the cuneiform writings is so like the stories of Azi-Dhaka or Bevarasp in the Bundehis and Astyages in Herodotus that the same chief is mentioned in all three. Moreover, it is evident that Bevarasp and Azi-Dhaka were dynastic titles and that Istuvegu was the name of the king to whom these titles were applied.

Herodotus was portrayed by the Astyages as a Median king, but inscriptions from Nabonidos, the King of Babylon, indicate that he was in charge of the Barbarian host, or "Tsab Manda." Still, this might have been no more than a slur intended to belittle. The Babylonian kings faced formidable opposition from Astyages and his ancestors. Kastarit, a.k.a. Cyaxares, was one of the chiefs who led the overthrow of Assyria. Moreover, one of Istuvegu's ancestors launched an assault on Babylonia. An old astronomical tablet records: 'The Tsab Manda comes and takes control of the area." The altars of the great gods are removed. Bel journeys to the land of Elam. Elam and Media bordered Ellipi, the main Astyage capital, and Media was unquestionably within his sphere of influence. His ancestor, Deiokes, founded the royal city of Ekbatana, also known as Agamtanu. Today, it is known as Hamadan. It appears that Deiokes subjugated the numerous tribes in the media. According to inscriptions from Nabonidos and Cyrus, the latter conquered Istuvegu. However, these records support the Bundehis' claim that an uprising helped the invader. Additionally, it mentions that the conqueror's own army delivered Istuvegu to him.

India Tanjavur Altar Goddess Naga with snakes

Firdusi makes a convincing case for the king's religious fervor and his support of the barbaric rituals and human sacrifices connected to serpent worship as reasons for the uprising. Or it might have been that, like Jemshid, Yima, and other Solar kings to be mentioned later, Istuvegu himself claimed divine honors as an incarnation of the Sun god and that the serpents that were said to have grown from his shoulders were those that formed the canopy over the head of his sculptured representation in his temple. Herodotus claims that the king was never seen in public. According to the Shahnama, the snakes that looked after Zahak, or Azi-Dhaka, had to be fed the brains of human victims on a daily basis. Gavah, the blacksmith, starts a rebellion after realizing that he would have to sacrifice his two sons, and Feridun takes advantage of it. Gavah's leather apron was used by the rebels as a banner, and centuries later, it was made sacred and used as such throughout Persia until the country was conquered by the Mohammedans.

As the above illustrates, up until the Astyates' reign, the kings of Media and the neighboring countries were serpent worshippers and went by the dynastic name of Azi-Dhaka. They all probably belonged to the same race or tribe as the Azi-Dhaka, who were said to have "sawed Yima in twain." Both Ahi and Azi, which signify serpent, were tribal or dynastic titles rather than given names. The Rig Veda makes no mention of Ahi being called Dhaka or that Vritra destroyed Yima, which is Yama in Hindu mythology. The Ahi of the Rig Veda and the Azi of the Zend Avesta most likely represent chiefs of the same widely dispersed Sun-worshipping people, even though their emblem was the many-headed serpent. The Danavas, sons of Danu, of the Rig Veda and the Mahabharata are, moreover, probably the same people as "the Turanian Danus of victorious strength," as mentioned in the Zend Avesta. Vritra the Ahi was one of their strongest chiefs, as we have already seen. Azi, from the Zend Avesta, is reported to have had three heads and six eyes. The Rig Veda similarly describes asura chiefs. We learn that "Thou, Lord (Indra), with six eyes and three heads, humbled and subdued the loud-shouting Dasa."

Additionally, according to the Satapatha Brahmana, Twashtri had a son named Visvarupa, who had three heads and six eyes and whom Indra killed. Visvarupa is also referred to as the great Asura or Mahabharata. In all these cases, the hoods of the protecting serpents expanded over the head of the Naga raja are certainly referred to; the passage just quoted from the Rig Veda is very significant because it demonstrates that the three Nagas of the epic poems were known to the Vedic rishis and were not a creation of later times. Zahak, or Azi-Dhaka, as mentioned earlier, is supposed to have had serpents growing from his shoulders; some of the sculptured representations of the Naga demigods in India have this appearance, but most of the time, the tail of the serpent is shown at the back of the figure, over the head of which its hoods are spread out. Vritra and Arbuda have been shown to have been Asuras, Danavas, and serpent chiefs; Namuchi, Urana, Sushna, Sambara, Pipru, and other Daityas and Danavas, whose struggles with Indra, or his followers, are the subject of so many Vedic hymns, appear to have been chiefs of tribes that opposed the Dharma.

Not drought, not climate change, but Aryas. Commentator Sayana asserts that influences today have human characteristics. Though this writer lived long after the events recorded in the hymns and was far from the scene of their occurrence, he was obviously misled by the figurative language of the Vedic rishis. Nevertheless, modern scholars seem less and less inclined to rely on the Brahman commentators. When viewed in the context of the previously quoted passages from the Rig Veda, the following verses make it abundantly evident that the battles fought against the Asuras were real fights, many of which were fought—or were thought to have been fought—in defense of the rishis or rajas, his devotees. For example, one hymn states, "Thou (Indra) didst hurl down the Dasa Sambara from the mountain; thou didst preserve Divodasa." And again, "Thou didst cast down the Dasa Sambara son of Kulitara from the great mountain."

Moreover, we have the following prayer: "Discriminate between the Aryas and those who are Dasyus, restraining those who perform no religious rites; compel them to submit to the performer of sacrifices." This refers to people rather than clouds. "Munificent hero, who easily conquers thy foes, thou did put to fight the Dasyus in battle." We are also told that "Indra shattered, for Divodasa, the hundred castles of Sambara." And once more: "Indra, wielder of the thunderbolt, warring on behalf of Purukutsa, thou didst overthrow the seven cities; thou didst cut off, for Sudas, the wealth of Anhas." In a different hymn, we have: "Benevolent to man, thou hast broken the cities of Pipru and protected Rijisvan in his battles with the Dasyus." Moreover, we read: "Thou didst break his castles; thou didst sweep away the wealth of Sushna." Moreover, we read that "Indra, in his might, quickly demolished all their strongholds and their seven cities." He has given Tritsu the son of Anu's dwelling; may we (by appeasing Indra) vanquish the unintelligent man in combat." The passages just quoted indicate that Asuras and Dasyus were, as depicted in the epic poems, the leaders of hostile tribes that opposed the Aryas, not demons or natural phenomena.

After considering all the evidence above, it is impossible to conclude otherwise than that the Asuras, Dasyus, Daityas, Danavas, and Serpas of the Rig Veda were the Nagas of the epic poems, and it is even less likely that the people who worshipped serpents and were called these names belonged to the same race as the tribes mentioned in the Zend Avesta, represented by the Azi and the sons of Danu. In fact, the mountains mentioned so frequently in the Rig Veda could only have existed before the Aryas or Devas crossed the Indus. Most of the Ahi's battles took place in the wild region of Afghanistan. The Naga demigods were the widely worshipped deities everywhere between Kabul and the Indus until the population was converted to Islam, and we will see in the future that serpent chiefs ruled Kabulistan during the early years of the Persian empire. The rulers of the neighboring state of Ghor claimed descent from the same race up until the time of the Mohammedan invasion. According to the Satapatha Brahmana, Vritra was a serpent and a Danava.

This "prince of the Daityas" was then "occupying the whole earth and the heavens," and the Mahabharata tells us that Vritra ruled over groups of vicious Danavas known as Kalakeyas, who were unbeatable in combat. Thus, like so many solar chiefs, Vritra claimed supreme authority and divine honors. The Sun, also called Vishnu, gave birth to the Kalakeyas, also called Kaleyas or Kalakhanjas, who lived in the Patalan region, which encompasses the Indus Valley and neighboring countries. In this domain of his dominions, Naga Rajas succeeded Vritra, the great Ahi; from the Mahabharata, we learn that the legendary Asura Arbuda was a Naga raja; from the genealogy of the solar race, we learn that Ahi Naga was the name of one of the Ajudhia royal families; and we also learn that Ahi Deva was a god worshipped in Kashmir. The Sun, or perhaps the Sun god, was the principal deity of the Asuras, from whom they believed they were descended, and they also worshipped the Naga, as we have seen in the case of the Kaleyas or a hooded snake, as The hood of one or more of these serpents spread over his head served as the totem or protector of their kind, identifying a Naga demigod or deified solar chief.

The depictions of Asura and Rahu, the Naga demigods Vasuki or Baska Naga, Indru Naga and other serpent deities, and Surya, the Hindu Sun-god, all have a canopy over their heads made of the hoods of seven-headed Nagas. Further evidence, though not necessary, will undoubtedly establish the connection between the Asuras, or Nagas, and the Indian branch of the solar race; the term "Naga" seems not to have been a tribal name but rather a designation by Brahmanical writers to identify those who worshipped the hooded serpent, or Naga; certainly all Asuras worshipped this snake, just as other people who claimed to be of Sun-descendant did. It appears to have been adopted before the division into tribes, which is thought to have resulted in the large number of totems that existed later. The Naga people hold it in such high regard that it is thought to be the original totem of the widely dispersed solar race. We find out that different tribes were identified with different totems or sub-totems and that these tribes belonged to the

Asuras or Nagas; all tribes, however, worshipped the Sun and believed in the Nag. Though Kasyapa had two wives, according to some Brahmanical authorities, Asuras and Aryas were descended from one of them. He was probably the sun god or one of the first solar chiefs to be deified, and together with the tortoise, he is regarded as the progenitor of the solar race. The Satapatha Brahmana tells us that this tortoise (Kasyapa) is the same as the sun. The tortoise was one of the most ancient and well-liked totems among the solar race.

Likely, the various animals, birds, reptiles, and other objects ascribed to Kasyapa as progeny represent the totems or sub-totems of different solar tribes. For good reason, Kasyapa has been linked to the tribes that inhabit the region south of the Caspian Sea. The Sea of Milk, known as the Kaspian, encircled Saka Dwipa, or the Scythian country, and is believed to be the location where the rishi Vrihaspati went to consult "the great Kasyapa." These verses speak to the myth that the Naga Rajas possessed the ability to control the elements, a myth that persists to this day. This power is thus mentioned in one of the Vedic hymns that describe a battle between Indra and Ahi, or Vritra: "When Indra and Ahi fought, neither the lightning nor the thunder (released by Vritra), nor the rain that he showered, nor the thunderbolt, hurt Indra." The Vedic hymns frequently mention the Asuras' denial of rain, especially that of the powerful chief Vritra, and how the ensuing drought ended when the enemy perished.

Since they believed that the Asura chiefs controlled the elements, it was only natural for the worshippers of Indra to turn to him for assistance when they experienced drought or a storm that they believed was a result of their enemies' influence. There are numerous tales in northern Indian folklore about the might of the Nagas. During dry spells or spells of heavy precipitation, these demigods continue to be worshipped before all other deities. It is said that during these earlier times, human sacrifices were frequent. Buddhist authors frequently allude to the Nagas' dominion over the elements. To terrify Naga raja Aravalo and convert him to the religion of Buddha, the Mahawanso recounts that when the hero Majahantiko was sent to Gandhara and Kashmir during the reign of Asoka, "the people remained unmoved, and the raja converted." However, the hero sparked a severe storm that included rain, thunder, lightning, and thunderbolts. The name for this dragon-like force that Chinese Buddhist pilgrims frequently mention is Naga power. Sung-Yun claims that Buddha traveled to Udyana to win over a Naga king who had let loose a deluge of rain in a fit of rage. Fah-Hian, written in 400 A.D., tells how the dragons of the Tsung-ling mountains created wind, rain, snow, and other natural phenomena. According to the same pilgrim, a friendly dragon at Sankisa produced fertilizing rain, and a Buddhist priest led worship at his temple. Hiouen-Tsiang discovered in the seventh century that the Takshasila people were accompanying Sramanas in a procession to the shrine of Elapattra Naga in order to pray for rain.

Even though their rulers are now Mohammedans, the people of the Hindu Kush states of Hunza and Nagar still believe they are powerful. This "power is still ascribed to the serpents" in the sun-worshiping countries of China, Manchuria, and Korea, at least until the advent of Christianity in Mexico and Peru. In Kashmir and many other parts of India, the sun or one or more of the Naga demigods held sacred sites for lakes and springs. Although the cobra is a water snake and cannot survive underwater, the Naga rajas were thought to possess the power to control the elements, particularly the waters, which likely resulted from their relationship with the sun. As a result, they were associated with springs, streams, and lakes where the serpent deities were thought to reside. Most Sun temples have nearby "Suraj Kund," or pools of the Sun, which the Sun god reveres. Numerous folktales depict the catastrophic storms and other misfortunes that ensue from the contamination of hallowed waters. There are also several pools and springs at Naga temples. There has always been a relationship between the sun, the sea, the serpent, rivers, lakes, and the waters themselves. Indian mythology portrays Vishnu, the sun god, as a multiheaded serpent supporting him as he floats above the ocean. The massive Martanda temple in Kashmir was constructed at a tirtha, or sacred spring, and was dedicated to the Sun-God Martanda, also known as Vishnu Surya.

Buddha and the Seven Naga

2. ASURAS AND NAGAS

Upon reaching the boundaries of India, the Aryas came across the Asuras, Dasyus, or Nagas, who were not your average aboriginal tribes, but rather highly developed societies complete with cities and fortresses. Some of these, according to the Veda, were made of stone. Indeed, it seemed that the Asuras had progressed beyond the level of the rival Aryan civilization. There were important locations in several of their cities, as we will see shortly. Brahmanical writers also connected the Asuras to luxury and wealth, magic, the power to raise the dead, and extraordinary building abilities. A portion of the magic was due to superior mechanical ability. The Aryas could have been more successful in their attempts to resurrect their enemies, but it took them a while to figure it out. It was most likely information about medications and operations. If not for the dead, then at least the ill and wounded could have been revived in this manner.

According to Brahmanical authority, we also learn that Sesha Naga taught the ancient sage Garga, one of the fathers of Indian astronomy, about planets, astronomy, and the good and evil represented by the aspects of the heavens in exchange for a sacrifice. The Nagas holds a very important position in Indian astronomy, and it is unlikely that their Brahmanical rivals gave them this ranks by accident. The Asuras brought this and other branches of science from their former homeland in the nations between the Caspian Sea and the Persian Gulf. The close relationship between the Chaldean and Indian astronomical systems has been noted numerous times. The Asuras worshipped the sun; the Naga, a hooded serpent sometimes pictured with many heads, was revered; kings and ancestors were deified; cedar was revered; religious dances were performed; sacrificial rites were performed; communication with the gods was facilitated by inspired prophets; there was an occasional tendency toward democratic institutions; the use of tribal emblems or totems was common; and many of their social customs seemed to connect them to that very early civilization, whether Turan or not. As a matter of fact, they had a great deal in common with the people who lived in ancient Babylonia and maybe even more with Elam and the surrounding countries.

As we shall see later, the Dravidians and the Asuras were one and the same people. Known as part of the Asuras' domain, some of the important and prosperous cities on or near the Indus were Patala, Pragjyotisha, Saubha, Hiranya-Pura, and Takshasila. The Asuras established Magadha, Mathara, and other cities in the Ganges valley very early on. Ujaini, also known as Visalapura, is Naga city. The Mahabharata describes the tirtha of Mani Naga as a revered site of pilgrimage that was well-known even at that early time. The Asuras' Brahmanical successors took control of it, as they did with other Asuras' holy places. Krishna points out to Arjuna the areas in the vicinity of Magadha where the Nagas Arbuda and Chakravapin, "those persecutors of all enemies," as well as "the Naga Swastika and that other excellent Naga called Mani," dwelt "of old." The Asura Madhu founded Mathara, also known as Madara, and it is believed that Satrughna, Rama's brother, inherited it from his son Lavana.

The same-named region, whose capital was Patala, has been a part of the dominions of the great Ahi Vritra, as was previously mentioned. The royal rishi Kapila Vasudeva, also known as Kapila Naga, oversaw Patala and destroyed the sons of Sagara. Ikshvaku, too, from whom so many Solar dynasties claim descent, was a raja of Patala. Since Sakya Buddha belonged to the solar race and was descended from Ikshvaku, Buddhist authorities were especially interested in these dynasties. One source state that Ikshvaku's descendants established nineteen capital cities: Kusa-Wati, Ayojapura, Baranasi, Kapila, Hatthipura, Ekachakra, Wajirawati, Madhura, Aritthapura Indapatta, Kosambi, Kanagochi, Roja, Champa, Mithila, Rajagaha, Takkasila, and Kusinara. From Patala and other nearby ports, the Asuras, also known as the Nagas, sent expeditions to raid or colonize the nearby coasts. Alexander later outfitted his fleet from this location as well. Krishna killed Salwa, the son of Daitya, near the water's edge after capturing Saubha, another Asura city. It is said that Pragjyotisha, called "the great and impregnable city of the Asuras," was captured and that the same Yadava hero killed its ruler, Naraka. Pragjyotisha's later chief, Bhagadatta, ruled the West like another Varuna, meaning that he claimed the sovereignty of the sea. Hiranyapura, the city of the great Asura Hiranyakasipu, and the scene of the man-lion avatar were, according to tradition, the present day Multan. The great temple of the sun in this city was celebrated throughout India from the earliest period until the time of the Muslim invaders.

Ancient Carvings of Nagas (half men, half snake deities)

The Vayu Purana mentions Taksha as a member of the Solar Race and the son of Bharata, Rama's brother; further proof that the Solar dynasties descended from Ikshvaku and were of Asura or Naga origin can be found in this. As we have just seen, Takshasila, the Taxila of the Greeks, was the capital of one of the Solar kingdoms founded by the race of Ikshvaku, and it was the city of Takshaka Naga. On his return from a raid into Takshasila, Janamejaya, the Bharata raja of Indraprastha, offered his serpent sacrifice at the behest of Brahman Utanka. The victims of this sacrifice, according to the Mahabharata, were the Naga prisoners taken during the raid, who were burned alive with Brahmanical rites. One of the most popular folktales in Punjab, the story of the serpent sacrifice is well-known throughout India. According to legend, an army of Nagas that invaded Indraprastha killed Raja Parikshit because the raja had kidnapped Basak Nag's daughter. Subsequently, the serpent sacrifice was carried out by his son, Janamejaya, who carried on the Nagas' extermination war. The Asuras, also known as the Nagas, were guardians of both banks of the great river Indus. They were not only a highly developed civilization but also powerful mariners; their early development of trade with the Persian Gulf must have resulted from their kinship with the serpent-worshipping people of ancient Media and the surrounding countries, as has already been mentioned.

"The Churning of the Ocean," which is only a metaphor for the earliest days of maritime trade, features the Asuras as major players. Rumored to have been used in "the churning process," the Mandara mountain probably represented a ship that Asian poets exaggeratedly and floridly described. The sea goddess Varuna's chariot is portrayed as being drawn by three-headed Nagas. Before the Aryas, or Devas could take part in the "Churning of the Ocean," they had to ask the Asuras for help. We then hear that Hari (Vishnu) gave the Devas instructions to make peace with the Daityas and promise to give them an equal share of the produce in order to win their cooperation in "churning the ocean." Devas and Nagas engaged in trade during the Manu era, which came after the one under discussion, and rules were set in that regard. On the other hand, it is likely Aryas and Dasyus's relationship changed dramatically, and the two people's union advanced significantly. If the Aryas had passed through the territory of their enemies at that time, they could have had access to the sea; the ships that the Rig Veda mentions in relation to the Aswins were probably Asuran vessels.

The sea is called the "home of the Asuras," the "habitation of the Nagas," and the "haven of the vanquished Asuras" in the Mahabharata. This is probably because the wandering bands of these people returned to their ships after a failed raid, so after Vritra died, "his followers sought refuge in the sea." When Krishna pursued him, the Patala-based Asura Panchajana did the same.

The Devas defeated the Danavas at the churning of the ocean, and so did they. The sons of Kadru eventually landed in the country of Ramaniaka on the coast of Malabar, where they encountered a strong storm and intense heat. This is according to an old legend found in the Mahabharata. Kadru, the mother of the serpents, forced Garuda to take her sons across the sea "to a beautiful country in a distant region, which was inhabited by Nagas." This region had previously been colonized by a fierce warrior named Lavana, an Asura of the same race. Consequently, Naga chiefs are often described as ruling countries in or under the sea; thus, the Naga raja Dhumavarna, whose kingdom was under the sea, took Yadu, the son of Hariaswa, who was the son of Ikshvaku and established Ratna-wipe (the land of gems), where the people traded and fished for pearls. Yadu married the jive daughters of the Naga chief in this island kingdom, which was most likely Ceylon. One of his sons, Harita, succeeded his grandfather.

After Ravana's army fled, Meghanada captured Indra and took him to Lanka, but she rallied them. Indra and his followers attacked Ravana, the strong raja of Lanka, or Ceylon. Rather than being a direct reference to Indra, it is more likely to be the inspired prophet, bearing the image or standard of god at the head of the army, as well as others where the gods are shown leading their followers in battle. We will discuss these prophets later. We find that on another occasion, Ravana attacked Arjuna Kartvirya's dominions on the banks of the Narbada and was himself captured; the invader in both cases could have reached his destination only by sea and would have needed a large naval arsenal to do so. These kinds of raids appear to have been frequent along the Indian coast, and similar descents were probably made on the shores of neighboring countries. It turns out that Patala was the residence of his grandfather and other family members. Son of Danu, his great-uncle Virupaksha was known as the great Asura in the Mahabharata. It has already been mentioned who the Dravidians and Asuras are. Ravana, though called a Rakshas in the Ramayana, was an Asura and probably the king of a Naga colony.

The Buddha himself claimed that the Virupakshas were a royal race of serpents, and that Virupaksha was the chief of serpents and regent of the West. The Grihya Sutras mention Virupaksha as a divine being entitled to worship. Certainly, the ten heads ascribed to Ravana were those of the guardian serpents, which, when he was a Naga raja, formed the canopy over his head; Usanas, the chief priest of the Asuras, or one of his offspring, oversaw the sacrifices made by Indrajit, the son of Ravana, who had a golden serpent as a device on his banner. From the preceding, it is evident that the Asuras possessed strong naval prowess and were adept navigators. They also founded colonies on distant coasts at a very young age, even prior to their alliance with the Aryas. The Naga demigods provided the Neptune trident, while the Asuras used the conch shell that the Tritons had used before them. But as was already mentioned, the Asuras were no different from some of the people living in the Persian Gulf, with whom they no doubt continued to communicate at sea. The Nagas' affinity for the ocean and nations beyond it suggests that they traveled to India by sea; however, their very early occupation of the Himalayan and Hindu Kush slopes, as well as northern India, contradicts this, as does their relationship with the serpent tribes of Kabulistan and further west, which has already been discussed and will be brought up again.

It is reported that the rishi Narada knew every Patalan, and he was obviously very fond of them all; the conflict between Aryas and Dasyus continued until the end of the Vedic era, with varying degrees of success; the Aryas seem to have allied themselves with one tribe at times and with another, and the Asuras seem to have been involved in numerous intertribal conflicts; we also find that the Rishis and other religious ascetics went to see both Devas and Asuras and that they both enjoyed each other's company. Over time, business agreements were formed, such as those mentioned in the folktale "The Churning of the Ocean." Since ancient times, intermarriages have happened even in the most esteemed circles: Indra's wife was the daughter of the Asura chief Puloman, and his daughter Jayanti wed Usanas, the chief priest of the Asuras; after that, the Naga Sumukha of the Airavata race wed his daughter Gunakesi to Matali, the "friend, counselor, and charioteer" of Indra.

There are numerous instances in the Mahabharata of Brahmans and Kshtriyas intermarrying with Asuras. Chief of the Nagas, Aryaka was the grandfather of Sura, king of the Surasenas, and father of Krishna's father, Vasudeva, and Pandu's wife, Kunti. The sons of Naga's mothers were Somasrava, the family priest of Pandava Raja Janamejaya, and Brahman Astika, whose influence prevented that monarch from offering snake sacrifices. This illustrates how close-knit Aryas and Asuras' family ties have become. Under these circumstances, the hostility between the two races would have waned, and the Rig Vedic demons would eventually have changed in appearance. This was indeed the case. Consequently, the Sama Veda describes Indra as having consumed the Soma of Kadru, the mother of the serpents, in full assembly, and the Aitareya Brahmana refers to Arbuda, the son of Kadru and an Asura warrior of the Rig Veda, as "the serpent rishi, framer of mantras." The fusion that happened between the Aryas and the Dasyus in India was comparable to the union that happened in Babylonia between the Semite and the Akkadian peoples.

The Naga snake Staircase

Three Naga demi-gods—Iravan, Dhritarashtra, and Takshaka Vaisalya—are mentioned in the Atharva Veda. In the Grihya Sutras, serpents are referred to as gods rather than enemies: "To the divine hosts of the serpents, Swaha! This is where the serpents are called Nagas. The Grihya Sutras state that serpent demi-gods Takshaka Vaisalya and Virupaksha are entitled to offerings made with the formula Swaha! The Paraskara Grihya Sutra, which instructs offering oblations to "the lord of the overpowering serpents belonging to Surya," fully confirms the relationship between the sun and the serpent. The passages just discussed show how much progress was made toward the union of the Devas and Asuras, as well as how the religion and attitudes of the Aryas changed significantly over time. The two people's slow fusion proceeded even as rival chiefs and antagonistic tribes kept fighting each other. The religion and way of life described in the Rig Veda had changed significantly by the time the epic poems were written. In addition, the distinction between Arya and Dasyu, or Deva and Asura, had all but disappeared, as they had all become Kshatriyas. Although some of them were still more orthodox than others, they all eventually went to Indra's heaven, and Swarga was shared equally and on equal terms by Devas and Nagas.

Takshaka was a Naga chief who lived with Indra in Swarga at the time of the serpent sacrifice. He was also regarded as the Devas' friend and benefactor. The term "Devas" is used in epic poems to refer to the living followers of Indra, such as the Aryas and the Aryanized tribes, in order to distinguish them from the unregenerate Asuras. The Devas are the souls of departed Kshatriyas and live with Indra in Swarga. We also learn that, during the time of the two races' union, Swarga was home to both Devas and Nagas. But since the warrior caste's souls were the Devas of Swarga, who are identified with the Pitris, this was merely a poetic rendering of the term. It is a widely held belief that, upon their deaths, Rajputs become Deos or Devas, a distinction that cannot be placed on any other caste. We also know that Sakra, the chief priest of the Asuras, separated himself through asceticism and became the spiritual mentor of both the Daityas and the Devas, in addition to the elements that united them. This demonstrates the connection between the Deva, or Arya, priesthood and the Asuran priesthood, which may account for some of the Vedic religion's changes and undoubtedly have a strong positive influence.

According to a hymn to Indra by the rishi Savya, son of Angiras, the Rig Veda seems to suggest a potential alliance between the two: "If Usanas should sharpen thy vigor by his own, then would thy might terrify, by its intensity, both heaven and earth." It is also said that Angiras's progeny had intermarriages with Bhrigu tribe members. Usanas, or Sakra, "lit fires, said mantras, and recited the Atharva Veda" to commemorate the Asuras' victory over Indra and to resurrect the Danavas, who had been killed in battle by the Devas. Bhrigu was the great rishi. It is also discovered that the spiritual mentors of the Daitya chief Hiranyakasipu were the Brahmans, sons of Bhargava (Bhrigu), distinguished priests, and reciters of the Sama Veda. Furthermore, we find out that after this Asura chief of Patala vanquished Indra and seized control of his kingdom, the descendants of Bhrigu, "Brahmans, declarers of the Veda," offered a hundred Aswamedhas for Bali. Thus, even though Bhrigu was acknowledged as a Brahman rishi, he was an Asura for a long time.

The marriage of Manu's daughter Arashi to Chyavana compelled Indra to grant the Aswins, or Dioscuri, a portion of the Soma. This implies that he undoubtedly brought these deities into worship. Bhrigu came by sea, as the Taittiriya Upanishad states that he was the son of the sea god Varuna. The fact that this rishi is also credited with being the father of the goddess Sri, also known as Lakshmi, most likely alludes to the fact that he brought devotion to that figure. This family of priests has, therefore, significantly influenced the modifications made to the Vedic religion. These gods were all transported from somewhere over the sea, probably the Persian Gulf coast. Like her Greek counterpart, the goddess Sri also arose from the "deep." They called the Aswins "ocean-born," and they had ships; she was one of the products of the "Churning of the Ocean." The sons of Bhrigu are said to have been reciters of the Sama and Atharva Vedas, as we have seen. The Sama Veda's Tandya Brahmana describes sacrifices, known as Vratyastoma, for the consecration of people who had not, up until then, adhered to the precepts of orthodox Brahmanism. These people were Kshatriyas based on the description given, and they were Asuras going through a regeneration phase. They carried bows and lances, drove war chariots, did not engage in trade or agriculture, and spoke an Orthodox language that was hard to pronounce.

This implies that a way to transform the Asuras has been discovered. The blending of the Dasyus and Aryas had also advanced significantly, with the adoption of a common language, among other things. The solar and lunar lines of the Kshatriyas were Asura-derived. As we have already seen, the Asura tribes claimed descent from the sun, but we also find that the moon is born from the sun. "Moreover, the Indian moon god Siva claimed possession of the moon when it arrived at the Churning of the Ocean. Though the rishi Atri is said to have been the father of the moon, it can hardly be argued that the Brahman Atri, who was apparently a son of Usanas, was the actual progenitor of the moon or of the Lunar line of Kshatriyas." This implies, undoubtedly, that the worship of the moon was either introduced or specially favored by this rishi, but the wards have been taken literally.

Large bronze snake deity

There are indications of this in the Mahabharata, where it is said that Atri killed the Asuras and assumed the forms of the sun and the moon god, Soma. There is little doubt that the introduction of moon god worship caused religious conflict among "the tribes." What became of the Lunar line of kings before the Brahmans deposed them for their evil deeds during the Pururavas' reign remains to be seen. Nahush was the son of Ayus of the Pururavas and Swarbhanu, the Asura chief's daughter. To replace Indra, this king made the Rishis carry his litter. He descended from heaven and, like his ancestors, took on the form of a Naga after mistreating the Brahmans and enslaving the Devas. Nahush is one of Kadru's sons and is mentioned among the Naga chiefs in the Mahabharata, according to the Harivansa. He is still regarded as Indra Naga.

The orthodox Yadu and Puru, the ancestors of the Mahabharata's heroes, were born to Yayati, son of Nahush. His wives were Devayani, the daughter of Usanas, the Asura priest, and Sarmishta, the daughter of the Daitya chief Vrishaparvan. Nahush and other kings had claimed divine honors before him. Probably for the benefit of the gods, this chief made the Brahmans carry his litter. This is clearly a long-standing combination of divinity and royalty, and the priestly caste seems to have come to terms with it. But when Nahush became too domineering, Arid kicked the rishi Agastya on the head to get him to move faster; this infuriated Agastya, who fell from heaven. To put it another way, the Brahmans organized a rebellion against him and overthrew him. These ancient kings, the sun god in human form, took the place of Indra. Prithu and Vena had declared their divinity before him. According to the Harivansa, the Sun god Vena challenged the Brahmans by stating, "It is to me that sacrifices should be presented, and oblations offered. If I will, I could burn up the earth or deluge it with water." It appears that the priests killed him or dealt with him in another way. Vena apparently claimed to have power over the elements.

When Prithu, a Chakra-various raja, succeeded him, it is said that Brahma perceived something of the Sun, or Vishnu, in him when he held the discus of Vishnu. We are also told that "the divine Vishnu (the Sun-god) entered the body of that monarch in consequence of his penances." It was also "for this reason that the entire universe offered divine worship to Prithu, numbered amongst the human gods" (demi-gods). It would seem, therefore, that during Prithu's lifetime, he was worshipped as the embodiment of the sun god. Moreover, the name Chakravarti Raja seems to have originated from the belief that the discus, or chakra, symbolizes both universal dominion and divine powers as the Sun god manifested. Prithu is still revered as one of the Naga demigods. Renowned Daitya leader Hiranyakasipu, the son of Kasyapa and Raja of Patala, claimed to have supernatural powers as well. It appears that the Brahmans in Bhrigu's family treated him like a god. Legend has it that Hiranyakasipu assumed the roles of the sun, moon, lord of the waters, air, and fire and usurped Indra's authority to rule the three worlds. Put another way, the kings of the solar race, including the Daitya chief, proclaimed their power over the elements. In his depiction, Vasuki is shown holding a discus or chakra with one hand, sometimes with both. Similar discussions serve as symbols for two other Naga demi-gods, Vishnu and the Sun god Surya.

The priests call the discus Vasuki Naga ka bhan. This and the discussion that Prithu was holding—the one that was just mentioned—represent the sun. In an extremely old Accadian poem, the Sun-God Merodach declares, "I bear the lofty weapon of my divinity, the Sun of fifty faces (rays?)." I am the lucky sun of my morning, the mountain-conquering hero." "My formidable weapon, which resembles an orb and strikes the fighters' corpses in a circle! I'm a bear. And again: "That which makes the light come forth like day, god of the East, my burning power, I bear." Furthermore, there is a clear reference to the sun or a picture of the sun in the following old hymn or poem: "The King, the shepherd of his people, may he hold the sun in his right hand; may he hold the moon in his left hand." It is clear from these passages that the picture of the Sun, either as an orb or a disk, held by the Sun god Marduk or Merodach and the early Babylonian kings was the same as the discus, chakra, or Naga ka bhan held by the Indian sun god Surya and the Naga rajas who claimed to be incarnations of the sun god. It was also likely the same as the disk that Brahma saw in the hand of Prithu, the Chakravarti raja, whom that god recognized as a person.

The Rig Veda describes how Indra killed Bala by spinning his vajra, or thunderbolt, in the same way that the sun rotates around his wheel. India, like Babylonia, represented the sun with a wheel or chakra. The Buddhist "wheel of the law" concept most likely originated from this wheel, or chakra of the sun. Another attribute of Krishna, who, as we shall see, claimed divine honors as an incarnation of the Sun god, was carrying a discus, which is sometimes portrayed as a symbol of his divinity and other times as a sharp weapon of destruction. At times, people likely mistook the disk of the Sun god for a sharp steel quoit, akin to those carried by Sikh martial devotees or Akalis. The Mahabharata has two different versions of how Pavaka, also called Agni, gave Krishna the discus, a weapon of fire; one version says it is made of iron. We find this again: "The chief of the Yadus, that slayer of all foes, in anger, instantly cut off the head of the ruler of Chedi by means of his discourse." Krishna then asserts that he initiated the great and powerful discus Sudarsana, "which reduced to ashes in battle, Yakshas, Rakshasas, Danavas, and kings born in impure tribes."

Seven snake heads (Sesh Nag) Angkor Wat, Siem Reap, Cambodia.

It is said that when Krishna passed away, his discus shot up into the sky. While the Puranic texts generally describe the Krishna discus as a cutting weapon, there are also stories of Sudarsana burning Kasi, slicing the Asura Naraka in half, and slicing the king of Paundraka into pieces. As previously stated, Krishna, like so many of the solar rajas, claimed divine honors as the sun god personified; however, Krishna was not a king but rather a deified hero, the younger son of a chief of the Yadavas, and he has now become one of the principal deities of the Hindu Pantheon, even exalting himself above Vishnu. Though Krishna claimed to be an incarnation of the sun god, it has been mentioned that the lunar line and the sun line were divided solely by religious differences rather than race. The Yadavas belonged to the lunar line of Kshatriyas. It is revealed that the Naga chief Aryaka, who belonged to the Kauravya or Kuru race, was great grandfathered by Krishna's father, Vasudeva. In addition, it is said that Balarama was an incarnation of Sesha Naga and that, on his death, his soul, shaped like a large serpent, leaped from his mouth. Balarama, the elder brother of Krishna, is depicted with multiple serpent hoods covering his head; this is presumably a reference to the serpent canopy that set the Naga rajas apart.

In the Bhagavad-Gita, Krishna describes himself as Vishnu among the Adityas, the sun that reverberates among bright bodies, the genius (or deity) in the solar disk, and the one who is the same as the Sun. As a result, other solar chiefs took the name Vasudeva, which Krishna had claimed, and destroyed that monarch's sixty thousand sons, who had invaded Patala in search of the horse. Chakradhanu, "who took his birth from Surya, and who was also known as Kapila or Kapila Vasudeva, and Kapila king of the Nagas, asserted his claim to universal dominion by seizing the sacrificial horse of Sagara." A rival known as "the heroic and mighty Vasudeva, King of Pundra" is reported to have adopted the name Vasudeva during Krishna's lifetime and to have "represented himself as a divine personage and to have borne the signs of a Vasudeva." It is also reported that this king claimed divine honors as the embodiment of the Sun god and that he saw himself as "the Vasudeva," who had come down to Earth before Krishna killed and defeated him. In fact, Krishna was their defender, and many of the chiefs who fought alongside him were called Asuras, probably the heads of tribes that were still unregenerate and had not yet absorbed Brahmanical philosophy. Krishna appears to have absorbed many Aryan traditions. He is described as washing the feet of the Brahmans, with whom he is friendly.

Among the kings despoiled by Krishna and his allies was the Naga raja of Takshasila, who lost Kurukshetra and the Khandava forest, that is, most of the land between the Sutlej and Jumna rivers. The eagle-shaped supernatural being, Garuda, supported Krishna in several of the battles above. In front of

Krishna temples, Vishnu is typically portrayed as an eagle with a human face or as a man with an eagle's head; this is a representation of Garuda, the vahana who carries Krishna. There is a list of 48 Garuda chiefs; it is said that only those who have distinguished themselves through strength, notoriety, and accomplishments are listed. The Mahabharata tells us that the Garudas lived in one of Patala's provinces and that they offered worship to Vishnu, also known as the Sun. Thus, the eagle, or Garuda, became the totem of one of the Solar tribes of Patala, who were fierce and warlike and who were always at odds with their neighbors. Legend has it that Garuda eats the Nishadas, rends apart the Yaksha corpses, and destroys the elephant and tortoise, which represent the solar tribes. Garuda is reported to have attacked Indra and taken Amrita hostage before obtaining a promise from the Nagas to provide for him, given his previous grievance that the Nishadas, or aborigines, on whom he had feasted, were insufficient.

Thus, the story of the eagle eating the serpents serves as a metaphor for conflict between tribes. The Garuda is said to have been distinguished by the auspicious sign known as "Srivatsa," which was also a special mark for Krishna. That chief led the Garudas and adopted their totem as his emblem, which is the source of the poetic description of Krishna riding on the eagle during his warlike expeditions. Various pieces of evidence have now shown that the Asuras, or Serpas, who were once part of the solar race, were the ancestors of the Nagas; this will help to explain the various legends related to the Nagas and Vishnu, the Sun, Garuda, and Krishna. However, Brahmanical writers depicted the Asuras as demons who had attacked the Devas in the same way that the Titans had attacked the Greek gods after the Devas and Danavas had all turned into Kshatriyas, and most of the earlier events had been forgotten. Subsequently, even further down the line, the Asuras changed into the Nagas of Patala, a region that is described as underground, and finally became Brahmanical Hell. The Solar tribes' descendants who had not experienced regeneration but had stuck to their ancestors' religion and customs were called Naga, and today, they are all devoted Hindus. However, Indian folklore abounds with tales of rajas and serpentine warriors; people commemorate the Naga demi-gods with festivals like Nagapanchami, which date back thousands of years.

Statue Of Nag Kanya on wall of Rani Ki Vav

3. VEDIC HYMNS

The differences between that period and the Vedic one has already been demonstrated. The epic poems portray the profound transformations in Indian society and religion. The Vedic and Mahabharata accounts of the religion are very different from modern orthodox Hinduism because further developments have taken place since the Epic era. Outside the Brahminic era, there have also been ups and downs in religious beliefs. The Buddhist religion has disappeared from India. Furthermore, a significant section of the population has been coerced into accepting Mohammed's religion. Despite all of this, though, "many of the ancient gods are still alive. The Sun, the cedar, and the serpent are revered; the Naga rajas are worshipped as gods; and Indra and his Devas still have their devotees and their temples, just as they did in the eras narrated in the epic poems.

Most of the Himalayan valleys and many other regions of India are home to these ancient, now-unorthodox deities. In the mountainous country bordering Kashmir, and especially in the tract lying between the Chenab and Ravi rivers, a remnant of the Nagas of the Mahabharata still survives. These people have remained under independent chiefs until comparatively recent times. They have escaped conversion to Islam, and they have saved their temples and their idols from the destructive zeal of Mohammedan iconoclasts, as well as from the almost equally destructive bigotry of the orthodox Brahman. Here, the serpent gods Sesha, Vasuki, Basdeo, Basak Nag, Takshaka or Takht Nag, and other Nagas less known to fame are still worshipped with their ancient rites. The forms of worship and the architecture of the temples have probably undergone little change since the days of the Mahabharata. And the serpent-gods are worshipped now, as they were then, not as dangerous reptiles nor as mere symbols, but as the deified rulers of an ancient people, who's tribal., or rather., perhaps, the racial emblem was the Naga or hooded serpent, and whose chief deity was the Sun.

These people do not call themselves Nagas. That term was not a tribal name but merely a distinctive term applied to those who revered the Naga, or hooded serpent. The name by which they are now known is Takha. Taxiles, Alexander's ally, was Takha raja.

It is not that all snakes are regarded with veneration; here, as elsewhere in India, the cobra alone is sacred. Other snakes may be killed without remorse. In one place only, as far as I am aware, worship is offered to any other serpent than the cobra. This is at the foot of the Rohtang Pass, where, under an overhanging rock, offerings are made to some small harmless snakes, which are called "Nag kiri." As this name shows, however, they are considered representatives of the Naga temples, however, are not dedicated to the serpent but to the Naga rajas, the human-form rulers of the race, such as Sesh Nag, Basak Nag, Takht Nag, Prithu Nag, Karkota Nag, Karsha Nag, Sabir Nag, Santan Nag, and many others; each, however, has the hoods of three, five, seven, or more serpents forming a canopy over his head, as Fergusson depicted in his plates of the Amaravati sculptures; in certain places, lesser-known Nagas are shown as men with snakes surrounding them but without the serpent canopy. There are also temples dedicated to Nagini Devis, who were the wives of Naga chiefs.

The Naga demigods' images in certain temples are covered in white calico, revealing only their heads. As previously mentioned, ever since the Asuras turned into Kshatriyas, their souls became Devas, and the souls of their wives became Devis. As a result, there haven't been any Nagas or Naginis recently; those whose shrines still stand are from a long time ago. Each temple contains the image of the Naga raja with the canopy of a serpent over his head; there are also numerous sculptures of stone and iron snakes, known as trisulas, and votive offerings left by worshippers; in addition, there is a lamp, an incense-burning dish, and the sacred iron scourge, known as sungal, Gaja, or iron scourge, which is the exact opposite of the one depicted in the hand of the Egyptian Osiris. In addition to the temples already mentioned, there are many small shrines with crassly carved images of serpents and similar images of the Naga under trees; all offerings were made. The Sun is a prominent feature at the Naga temples, where it is carved on the roof and other parts of the building.

I could find no evidence of any relationship between the Naga and the Phallus in these archaic shrines; the worship here is that of the Naga demigods, as descendants of the Sun and ancestors of the solar race; the Devas, too, are deified Kshatriyas and people's ancestors; the rituals and ceremonies performed at the Naga temples are essentially the same as those performed at the Devas' temples throughout the Himalayan region.

Additionally, it is extremely unlikely that anything significant has changed in this regard since the ancient times when the Nagas and the Devas occupied Swarga. In each case, goats and sheep are sacrificed, votive offerings are made, lights and incense are burned, the smoke of cedar is used for purification and protection against evil spirits, circumambulation of the temple takes place, and the deity is consulted through his inspired prophet. This representative of the deity sometimes passes through the fire or inhales the smoke of burning cedar and almost always does penance with the sungal or iron scourge.

Music and dancing form an important part of the ceremony. The musicians, who are often of aboriginal race and, therefore, considered to be of a lower caste, are not allowed to approach within a certain distance from the shrine. The dancing at the temples and in ceremonial processions is restricted to men. I had seen worshippers dancing before the litter, in which the representation of the deity was traveling, as David danced before the Ark. Aside from the Naga raja, in most of the temples dedicated to Vasuki or Basdeo in the Chenab valley, one finds a representation of his Wuzir, also known as Jimuta-vahana. According to legend, the Naga chief once narrowly escaped capture by the enemy while Basdeo and Garuda were at war; in actuality, his minister's devotion—giving his own life to save his master's—was the only thing that kept him alive. This suggests that Jimuta-vahana was slain in the process of covering the Raja's retreat. Basdeo managed to flee to the Kailas Kund, a mountain lake situated between the Chenab and Ravi valleys, approximately 131,000 feet above sea level. In the meantime, an army was raised, and Garuda was vanquished. The Naga raja gratefully commanded that Jimuta-vahana be worshipped in the same temple as himself going forward.

Vasuki, like other solar kings, was bestowed with divine honors during his reign. The legend, as just referred to, seems to relate to some of the struggles between the unregenerate and the Aryan tribes. It is probably founded on fact. Every year, the Kailas Kund hosts a sizable festival that is open to all residents of the region. It seems probable that this legend suggested the story of Jimuta-vahana in the Katha Sarit Sagara and the plot of the Naga Nanda, which is, in fact, the same story dramatized. In each case, the events occur during the reign of Vasuki; in each case, the name of the hero is Jimuta-Vahana; in each case, his home is in the Himalayas; and in each case, he gives himself up to Garuda to save the life of another. Here, however, the resemblance ceases. The drama has a Buddhist complexion. According to the representation, Vasuki must give Garuda one of his subjects every day to eat. The place of one of the victims is taken by Jimuta-vahana, who is partially devoured. Garuda then finds out his mistake, releases him, promises to eat no more human beings, and restores to life the Nagas he had previously consumed. Regarding this matter, it is noteworthy that the great Raja Siladitya, according to the Chinese Buddhist pilgrim I-tsing, entertained all the greatest writers, particularly poets, at his court and even participated in their recitals; the king would assume the role of Jimuta-vahana and change into a Naga amidst melodies and instrumental accompaniment.

I have not come across any representation of Jimuta-vahana in any of the many Naga temples in Garhwal and Kumaon, so the legend is local. As was previously mentioned, in a few of his temples, Basdeo or Vasuki is shown clutching a disc or chakra in one or both of his hands—a representation known by the priests as "Naga ka Bhanu"—while Surya, the Sun god, is shown holding an identical object. Thus, there are also other Naga Rajas and Indru Nagas (Nahush). This disc unmistakably represents the Sun. The majority of the Naga rajas' temples are constructed from enormous cedar logs and are situated within lovely, old cedar groves. Sadly, many the largest trees in the Chenab Valley were recently chopped down to make way for railroad sleepers. In the Hindu Kush and the Himalayas, as it was in ancient Babylonia and the surrounding nations, the cedar, also known as the kelu or deodara (tree of the gods), is revered.

After burning the branches of the tree as sacrifices, the inspired prophets breathe in the smoke, hoping to ward off evil spirits. Cedar was revered not only by the people of the hills; at Yudhishthira's great horse sacrifice, two of the sacrificial posts were made of deodara. Two of the posts at the Aswamedha of Dasaratha were also made of this holy tree. In both instances, the wood had to have been imported from the Himalayas because cedar does not grow in India's plains. This tree is so highly revered that, a few years ago, the people of Mandi, in the Beas valley, rose up in rebellion when the Raja leased a company of contractors the right to cut down deodar trees in his dominions. They said that although the trees belonged to the gods, the land certainly belonged to the Rajas. The Raja was forced to request protection from his enraged subjects from the British government. The Kashmir shawl pattern traditionally represents the cedrus deodara. In the Himalayas, other trees are considered sacred, such as juniper and ash, but none are revered as much as cedars. The various serpent-gods attend each other's festivals accompanied by their priests and office-bearers and wearing their respective insignias. In the same manner, the devas also pay each other visits. These festivals take place at every major temple. Usually, there's an open grassy space in front of them with chairs arranged like an amphitheater. According to old customs, every caste and family has a designated place.

Lord Vishnu on Adi Shesha at Badami Cave Temple 3.

In addition to the regular festivals, people congregate at the temples for other significant occasions, such as when they consult their gods through the inspired prophets. These gatherings typically take place during times of famine, war, or pestilence. Occasionally, delegates from the temples of different deities convene in a conclave. The Mahabharata passage that describes how the gods (Devas) gathered on the banks of the Saraswati and installed the excellent Naga Vasuki as king of all the serpents most likely alludes to such a convocation. Regardless of whether they are serving the Nagas or the Devas, the priests of most of these temples are Kshatriyas or Khuttris, as they are known locally. This is a remnant of long-gone traditions from the distant past when the Kshatriya chief made his own offerings.

Yet, the priests in a few of the temples are so-called "desi," or native Brahmans. None of the known Brahmanical clans acknowledge these, and they are not associated with them. They most likely come from families that have earned priestly dignity through their long history of involvement with the temples. They have intermarried with the Khuttris in many places. But in this, all they do is emulate the old rishis, like Sakra and Chyavana. It is extremely rare to find orthodox Brahmans serving as priests at these nonorthodox temples. The Brahman's position is subservient when it does occur. Regardless of the existence of a Brahman priest or not, the conduit for communication between the divine and the populace is invariably an inspired prophet. When a large portion of the worshippers are from lower castes or are descended from Aboriginal people, there may also be a lower caste prophet, known as a "lamahata," who relays to them the messages conveyed by the inspired representative of the deity.

It is known who inspired the prophet. By several names, including dharmi, dangariah, banahata, Chela, gur-chela, and, occasionally, as Ra. In general, he is a Kshatriya. On rare occasions, however, he is a desi-Brahman. Although I have never witnessed an orthodox Brahman act in this manner, I have witnessed one of them in the guise of a priest incensing the Chela while in a state of inspired fury. The Chela or banahata are not chosen; rather, they are meant to be "seized," or possessed, by God. If he is thought to be unfit, however, the village elders summon him before them, and in a serious meeting, they decide whether to accept his claims. The position is not inherited. When Chela receives his call, he must live a celibate life, sleep on the ground, avoid wearing shoes, and separate from his family. He also has to eat only food that he has prepared himself. Chela is permitted to live in his own home in certain circumstances, but the other regulations are upheld consistently. In most cases, no one else should touch Chela while she is under the influence of a deity. When, as is seldom the case, here, a Brahman priest is responsible for leading worship in a Naga or Deva temple; he is not in charge of the Chela, the temple's property, nor does he have the power to dictate to the worshippers what they must do or how the festivals should be observed.

The prophet, while under the influence of the divine afflatus, announced that the council of elders, guided by the will of the deity, is in charge of managing the temple. Then, the Chela is referred to as the deity and serves as its representation. The inspired prophet's words are likely mentioned when we read about Indra's or other gods' commands in the epic poems. As can be expected, these men have a significant impact, both positively and negatively. There is little doubt that the apparently inexplicable outburst of fanaticism is a result of these prophets' ravages. Sir G. Robertson asserted that the inspired prophets known as "pshurs" in the Hindu Kush valleys were to blame for a bloody war between two Kafir clans. I believe there was a similar reason behind the insane attack on a British force in Manipur a few years ago, which resulted in the deaths of multiple officers. At the very least, it seems likely. No one dared to disobey the orders given by the deity through the inspired Chela, a very intelligent chief assured me. If someone did that, he continued, a terrible disaster would undoubtedly occur.

Whatever his title in the local language, the inspired prophet at the temples of Devas or Nagas in the Himalayas is neither a magician nor a sorcerer. He does not claim to have any authority over the divinity he represents or any other, unlike the orthodox Brahman, either as a result of his austerities, through mantras, or through any rites or ceremonies. He is only God's spokesperson. To the best of my knowledge, the Chela is devoid of extravagant attire or hideous accessories. He dresses in the same manner as the other villagers, but he is not allowed to wear shoes. The chelas of some Devis and some Nagas, on the other hand, wear a red cap. This and the other villagers are of the same shape. The color is the only distinction. Naturally, the prophet received a great deal of respect, but his benefits were quite meager. Every victim who is sacrificed has the right to have their head taken; occasionally, they even get an additional portion. During harvest season, he also frequently receives small donations of grain, and if the temple has an endowment, he also gets a mall sum from that sou. Nonetheless, he typically gets the majority of his sustenance from his own land.

The information provided above does not entirely align with accounts of unconventional ceremonies "performed in the south of India." I am not familiar with these practices, so what I have just mentioned should be interpreted as exclusively pertaining to Northern India. I have known a number of these men, and while it would be oversimplifying to suggest that all of them have faith in their own intuition, I once "asked a man, whose father had been a chela, why he had not been inspired." The devil, he claimed, had never visited him. He didn't appear to question the possibility of his own inspiration or the truth of his father's. Regarding the devotees, the severity of their penances frequently reveals the sincerity of their faith. The punishment was the worst I have ever seen. I have witnessed a man apply the sungal, or iron scourge, to his own bare back and shoulders until the blood ran down in streams and formed a pool on the ground." As previously stated, Chela inhales the smoke of burning cedar, and occasionally, he drinks the warm blood from the beheaded victim's neck; he also occasionally jumps into or over the sacrificial fire, which he always applies to his own back, and occasionally, the worshippers' backs (the iron scourge mentioned earlier).Sometimes, this signal application to the worshippers' backs is just a ceremonial act, with no bloodshed; when the penitents apply the scourge themselves, the punishment is very severe.

As previously mentioned, this scourge is an exact replica of the one depicted in the hands of Osiris and several other Egyptian deities. It is made entirely of iron and weighs three to five pounds. It usually has three lashes, but sometimes there are five. The "aspaheastra," or "sraoshocharana," used by the Zoroastrians, is akin to the broad piece of leather at the end of a Tartar whip. Each lash is made up of two or three long links and a broad lancet-shaped blade at the extremity. But as I mentioned this to the late, great Professor Darmesteter, he believed that the Zoroastrian scourge wore leather thongs. It appears likely that they were different forms of the same instrument, applied in each case with the same technique and expiatory effect. A while back, the Chak, the Barmaor local chief in the Ravi Valley, invited me to witness a significant sacrifice to Kailang Nag. Stormy weather caused the sowing to be delayed, but the sacrifice helped. When I arrived, I noticed that everyone was gathered in the open grassy area in front of the temple, with the women and girls seated a little apart from the men. Kailang, like other Naga demigods, is supposed to control the weather. Just then, some of the boys and men began to dance in a circle, with the Chela at the center, as music began to play.

The music eventually brightened, and the dance intensified, with some of the men stopping to rest when they grew weary and the chela dancing despite using a similar scourge to scour his own back and shoulders as well as those of some of the other dancers. Then, to the cry of "Kailang Maharaj ki jai!" (Victory to the great King Kailang), some of the men applied another similar scourge to their own backs, with great effect. When everything was prepared, the victim—a ram—was led outside, and after demonstrating to God that it was okay by shivering, its head was severed. There were more shouts of "Kailang Maharaj ki jai!" as the body was immediately lifted by several men, the Chela grabbing it and drinking the blood that spurted from the neck, the head placed before the threshold of the temple with burning coal on it, and the carcass thrown to the ground. Subsequently, the dancing continued and intensified until the Chela exhaled Kailang Aya's (Kailang has arrived)." At that moment, all sounds stopped. An exclamation of "Kailang Maharaj ki jai! "" erupted when the prophet declared that the sacrifice had been accepted and that the season would be auspicious. and the weary Chela collapsed to the earth. He was covered in water and vigorously fanned until he began to show signs of life again. Then, the gathering started to break up.

Among the gods to whom human sacrifices have supposedly been made in the past is Kailang Nag. The Himalayas are home to numerous temples where it is rumored that human sacrifices were made during periods of drought and impending starvation. Certain villages provided the victims, and one of these, close to the Saeli Pass, is dedicated to a Nagini known as "Arna Naga," who has the reputation of having frequently refused to give rain" until she had eaten men.In the Chandra-Bhaga river valley, Kailang Nag had a shrine. There was a custom of offering human sacrifices. It was eventually decided to hold the sacrifice on the following day, and although there was a large crowd and the monk was present, he stated that he would stay at the temple until the deity came to devour him and that he would only die at the hands of the Naga. Eventually, it was time to provide for the victim, a widow with an only son, who was devoted as a result. A Buddhist monk noticed the mother, who was sitting close to the temple in a state of great distress. After hearing her story, he offered to step in for the victim. This was decided upon, and the monk persuaded the people that the Naga were against the sacrifice of men after sitting there for several days without being harmed. As a result, Kailang was no longer offered any human victims.

Like the Catholic Church, these temples accept votive offerings, which can be made to Devas or Nagas. Typically, these offerings are little models; occasionally, though, the object to which the offering is made is given up to the deity. I saw a spinning wheel in a tiny shrine that could hardly have accommodated it. Offerings are made to the gods rather than the Brahmans in this traditional form of Hinduism. These are the results of promises kept during illness, peril, or bad luck. For example, a man might pledge a trident to Vasuki or Tak-shaka, or a plow, a sword, or a bullock-yoke to the village's tutelary Deva. Most old temples have a number of stone tablets, resembling little tombstones, surrounding them; these are the memorials of departed villagers and are comparable to the gravestones in our churchyards, where the dead are burnt and there are no graves. A crudely carved image of a man or a man and woman can be found on each of these tablets.

Odisha style Hindu temple gate adorned with garlanded lady sculpture with multi headed snake as protection.

Occasionally, similar memorials honoring the wealthy villagers are built at the village spring, at a stream crossing, or in another well-visited spot. A resting place for travelers, a fountain, or a bridge over a stream are examples of public works of utility that are occasionally built in addition to the tablet. The Raja monuments are larger in scale and once depicted the wives and dependents of the chief who accompanied him to the afterlife. Some of the Devas' temples also have a pole or mast known as dhuj (dhwaja). This pine tree is bare of its branches, and each year it is replaced by a new one that is burned. This is the deity's standard, as its name implies. Indra gives the King of Chedi the order to erect an Indra Khwaja in the Mahabharata. The Chela frequently carries a smaller dhuj during processions. The boatmen on the Indus and other Panjab rivers place a pole at the bows or mastheads of their vessels as the dhuj of Khwaja Khizr, the Mussulman name for Varuna, the ancient sea goddess. Along with the temples of the Devis and Naginis, pilgrims also go to the temples of the Devas and Nagas.

These are usually performed at night by married men without children as a way of fulfilling their vows or to ask the deity for a favor; at several places, it is customary to mark the completion of the pilgrimage (called "likhnu") by drawing a line, every few yards, on a stone or other object by the side of the road; these marks are made with a mixture of rice flour and water and serve as a record that the pilgrimage has been completed. As previously mentioned, the Naginis were the wives of the Naga rajas; the Devis were, for the most part, the wives of Kshatriya chiefs who either became "sati" or were burned with the bodies of their husbands; today, however, the term is applied to almost all female divinities. These Devas and Nagas were the ancestors of modern Hindus; they were the well-known deities of the epic poems and the early Buddhist legends; Indra ruled over them and continues to do so in the Himalayas; however, orthodox Brahman now regard them as demons, and European writers who drew their information from Brahmanical sources have described them; the worship of ancestors, that is, of deified humans, has prevailed.

The worshippers of the Sun and the serpent, whose religious rites and ceremonies have just been described, are a remnant of a tribe, or group of tribes, once very powerful but now broken and scattered. Along with other variations, they are well-known in a variety of places, including Takha, Katha, Kathak, Kathia, Kathuria, and Kator. A few of these name changes result from the inversion technique, which is very prevalent in northern Indian dialects. For example, the name Lucknow is rendered as Nuklow in common parlance. In the Panjab, in the valleys of the Chinab, Ravi, and Beas rivers, live the majority of the Takhas, who still go by that name and worship their ancestors, the Naga demi-gods. Many of these handsome men are serving in our Indian regiments. They have always provided the majority of the recruits for the Kashmiri armies. There is nothing that sets the Takhas apart from other Rajput tribes in Punjab in terms of speech or physical appearance. They are among the thirty-six royal races of India mentioned by the bard Chand. The Takhas were not the only ones who worshipped the Naga. As was already mentioned, the hooded serpent was highly revered by all those who professed to be of solar descent.

However, among the Indian peoples who adhered to their ancestors' religion and customs, the Takhas were among the most powerful and dispersed. According to the Mahabharata, Takshaka, the legendary Naga chief, and his son, the powerful Aswasena, resided in Kurukshetra and Khandhava, with Takshasila serving as their northern capital. However, Takshaka is also known as Takshaka Vaisfiliya, and it is believed that this city was a part of his dominions because it is from Visala or Ujaini. In actuality, the Takha chiefs' dominion has spread throughout Sind, Punjab, the Hindu Kush, the Himalaya, and a sizable portion of what is now known as Raj Putana. The majority of these items were lost a long time ago. Local tradition states that the Takhas of Punjab held the Himalayas from the Indus to the Sutlej. The last Takha chiefs, to whom a semblance of independence remained, held out in the Chinab valley until Golab Sing of Kashmir drove them out. This is demonstrated by the numerous Naga demi-god shrines that can be found there as well as the numerous ruins of old fortifications that the locals credit to Takha chiefs, who are thought to have ruled the country before the rajas.

This was intended prior to the current Rajput families holding power. A significant portion of this tract is still under the control of the Takhas, and the ancient Takari alphabet, named after these people, is still in use from Bamian and the Kabul Alley to Nepal. In the seventh century, the Chinese pilgrim Hiouen Tsiang established the kingdom of Takha, which stretched from the Indus to the Beas and included the cities of Sakala and Multan. Additionally, the Chuchnama informs us that Jaisya, son of Dahir, king of Sind, fled to Takhia in the eighth and a half century after defeating Alakhana, king of Gurjara or Guzrat, and seized Takha, which was then a part of his dominions. Shankara Varma, king of Kashmir, defeated Alakhana early in the tenth century. The Takha chief was granted back control of the country, and he became dependent on Kashmir. In addition to the Takha kingdom in the Himalayas, which, as previously mentioned, stretched from Kashmir to the Sutlej, the region west of the Indus, all the way to Kabul, was governed by a subset of the same people, commonly referred to as Kator, who will be discussed later.

Detail of an ancient wooden carving, the snake goddess, Southern India

The region from the Sutlej to Nepal was once again inhabited by a different branch of the same race known as Katir, Kathuria, or Kathiur. The Kathurias, like the Takhas or Kathas, claimed descent from the Sun through the Naga demi-gods. The most ancient temple at Josimath, in the Alaknanda valley, which was the residence of the early Kathuria rajas, is dedicated to Basdeo, as the ancestor of the Kathurias. The Takari alphabet was and is still used in Garhwal and Kamaon, as well as the temples of the Naga demi-gods, which But Takshaka is replaced by Airi, or Airavata. This may be because Takshaka was a chief of Punjab, and "the serpents, subjects of King Airavata, splendid in battle," appear to have resided on the Ganges' northern bank, where numerous Naga dwelling places are rumored to exist. The trisul, or trident, is the symbol of Airi, as it is for other Naga demi-gods; shrines to Devas are also common in Gurhwal and Kamaon; the rites and ceremonial practices observed at the shrines, both of Devas and Nagas, are like those used in the worship of these deities in the Panjab, which have already been described.

A local legend states that Sankara Acharya, who had a large following when he arrived from the Dekhan, was well-received by one of the Kathuria rajas, and with his help, drove the Buddhists out of Gurhwal, Kamaon, and Nepal. The most significant religious institutions were then turned over to Sankara's followers, whose descendants continue to this day. The annals of Nepal fully confirm the Kamaon legends a Furthermore, the massive Vishnu temple at Badarinath is said to have been built by the Raja for the Brahmanical reformer. The principal priests of this temple, including the Rawal, are still Namburi Brahmans from southern India. According to legend, Sankara promised the Raja that he would not eat or drink until one hundred temples dedicated to Vishnu had been constructed. The Raja issued the required directives, and the temples were constructed in clusters. Some of the Kathuria rajas, like other Solar chiefs mentioned, seem to have taken on the title of Vasudeva or Basdeo, and they probably also claimed the divine honors that belonged to it.

They are still standing, but it is said that the majority of them were never used for worship. In an inscription in the old temple to Basdeo at Josimath, one of the Kathuria rajas is called "Sri Basdeo Giriraj Chakra Churamani. Several sources mention that Rajpal, the Raja of Indraprastha or Delhi, invaded Kamaon, where a chief by the name of Sakwanta or Shakaditya defeated and killed him. The conqueror seized upon Indraprastha and reigned there for fourteen years. Vikramaditya, whose capital was Ujaini, then overthrew and killed him. Sakwanta was apparently one of the Kathurias, who had then been rulers of Kama. For a very long period, as we shall presently see, Basdeo, a conqueror from Kamaon, the country of Kuttair, seized the throne of Kanoj during the period of anarchy that followed the passing of Raja Bhoj Puar. Who this Basdeo was is still being determined. However, as he came from Kamaon, he probably was one of the Kathurias. Basdeo is said to have reigned at Kanoj for seventy years. At his death, his sons quarreled over the succession, and Ramdeo Rhator, who had been commander of the army of Basdeo, seized the throne. After some time, Ramdeo attacked the Sawalik chiefs.

He was opposed by the Raja of Kamaon, who "had inherited his country and ·his throne from a long line of ancestors who had reigned upwards of two thousand years." In a great battle that lasted from sunrise to sunset, the Kamaon raja was defeated and fled to the hills. Ramdeo, having compelled him to give his daughter in marriage, left the Raja in possession of his country. The Kathuria dynasty continued to rule in Kamaon for many generations after this, for an inscription was found at Dwara of Ananta Pala Deva Katifir, the date of which corresponded to A.D. 1122. Some minor chiefs who claim descent from the Kathurias remain. All ancient remains in Gurhwal and Kamaon are ascribed by the people to this dynasty, and several of the former chiefs of this line are still worshipped as Devas.

Sculpture of Hindu God Vishnu laying on 5 headed Snake

Bas-relief of a half woman half snake, Nepal

4. ANCIENT NAGA CITIES

The people with whom Alexander first came into contact after crossing the Indus were the serpent worshipping Takhas or Kathas. The Taxila of the Greeks was the ancient Naga capital, Taksliasila, and, as already mentioned, Taxiles, or Omphis, was a Takha chief. Takhas, or Kathas, are still the principal land-holders in the country around the ruins of the great Naga city, which is locally known as Katha-des. These people, who are now Mohammedans, maintained a state of semi-independence until comparatively recent times. Adjoining the territory of Takshasila to the north and east were the serpent-worshipping countries of Uraga, or Urasa, and Abissara. Beyond these was Kashmir. This country was, according to its own historians, under the protection of Nila Naga and other serpent deities from the earliest times. One of the principal dynasties, which afterward ruled Kashmir, was descended from the Naga demi-god Karkotaka. Every spring, stream, and lake in this country was sacred to one or other of the Naga deities. Abul Fuzl tells us that in seven hundred places, representations of the serpent gods, carved in stone, were set up and worshipped.

At the same time, according to the same authority, there were only forty-five shrines sacred to Siva, sixty-four to Vishnu, three to Brahma, and twenty-two to Durgah. The Naga demi-gods, therefore, were by far the most popular deities. The sites still bear the names of the serpent deities to whom the sculptures were sacred, despite Mohammedan iconoclasts having destroyed them. In almost all of the neighboring Hindu states, the people are of the solar race, and the Naga demi-gods are worshipped as ancestral deities. We have already seen that tribes known as Ahi, or serpents, opposed the Aryas, or Devas, on the borders of India during Vedic times. Additionally, we have seen that these appear to be members of the Azi-Dhaka race of the Zend Avesta. At a later period, we find descendants of this serpent race still ruling in Kabul and in the neighboring country as tributaries of the Persian empire.

We learn from Firdusi, who receives confirmation from Mirkhond and other Persian authorities, that Zal, son of Sam, who ruled Zabulistan under the king of Persia, paid a visit to Mihrab, the chief of Kabulistan, who was a member of the Zahak family.

Zal fell in love with Rudabeh, the daughter of Mihrab, but the Mobeds, or Zoroastrian priests, who were consulted, knowing that Mihrab was of the serpent race, would not sanction the marriage. The matter was referred to Sam. This chief does not seem to have made any objection, and his influence was sufficient to obtain the consent of the Persian king, although that ruler had previously ordered the destruction of Kabul by fire and sword and the slaughter of the descendants of Zahak. The great Persian hero Rustam was the son of Zal, and his mother was Rudaheh, the daughter of the serpent chief. Mirkhond, in describing Rustam's relationship with the chief of Kabulistan, says that, consequently, Rustam was called "Kabuli" by the nobles at the Persian court. After Rustam died in Kabul, his son Ferimarz took over as ruler of Kabul and Zabul. Ferimarz held the position until the Persian king assassinated him. Up until relatively recently, descendants of Azi or Zahak lived in other parts of the mountainous nation that is now known as Afghanistan. Malcolm, in his history of Persia, says that the princes of Ghor derived their proud descent from Zahak and boasted that their ancestors had successfully opposed Feridun.

Ferishta tells us that "the race of Zahak, one after another, succeeded to the chieftainship of Ghor until the time of the Prophet." Additionally, we learn from the same source that the most reliable historians believed it was possible to trace the ancestry of the Ghor kings upward by using their names for between three and twenty generations. Minhajus Siraj, who came from Ghor to India in A.H. 624 (A.D. 1227) and whose father was Kazi to the army of the great Mahomed Ghori, commences his history of the Ghorian kings with a genealogical list that traces their descent back through Zahak to Noah. Whatever may be thought of this long pedigree, there was evidently a general agreement among historians that the kings of Ghor, in the mountains of Afghanistan, were descended from Zahak. The ruling family of Kabul, in the time of Rustam, and the chiefs of Ghor, as late as the thirteenth century, claimed to be of the serpent race. So in the principal states of Afghanistan, that is, the very country in which the Aryas encountered Ahi, the serpent chief of the Rig Veda, the ruling families claimed to be descended from Azi, the serpent chief of the Zend Avesta. We shall see later that the people of the country between Kabul and Kashmir, down to the time of the Mohammedan invasion, still worshipped the Naga demi-gods.

A beautiful shiva miniature statue in Nataraja pose guarded by a Naag

In the Pahlavi Karnam-i Artakshir-i Papakan, it is mentioned that the Persian King Artakshir, in the first half of the third century, was defeated more than once, and his camp was taken by Haftan Bokht. This chief, who was ruler of Kirman and lord of the dragon, worm, or serpent, was eventually defeated and killed. The ruins of his fortress of Guzaran are near the town of Barn, not far from the frontier of Baluchistan. The Barn Fort is still known as Kut-i-Kirm, the Fort of the Worm, or Serpent. Other traces of the serpent race remain in the neighboring country. In Baluchistan is the Koh-i-Maran, or the mountain of serpents, which doubtless took its name from the race of Zahak. According to one of the legends surrounding the construction of Herat, Zahak's daughter founded this fortress. Notwithstanding the conversion of the people to the Mohammedan faith, traditions connected with the serpent race still remain in the wild country between Persia and the Indian border. Near Mazar, in northern Afghanistan, is the village of Gor-i-Mar, or grave of the serpent, where a great. According to reports, Ali killed the serpent. Amongst the Kafirs of the Hindu Kush, there is also a tradition that the Bashgul valley was once held by a great serpent, who devoured travelers passing that way and who was killed by Imra or Indra.

The first clear descriptions we have of the country between Kabul and the Indus are those of the Chinese pilgrims who visited India as the holy land of Buddhism. Of these, Fah Rian arrived in India about A.D. 400 and seems to have traveled by way of Balti and the upper Indus valley. This pilgrim says: " Crossing the river Sinto (Indus), we come to Wuchang, where commences Northern India. "Wuchang, or Udyana, included the valley of the Swat River and much of the neighboring country. Fah Hian continues by stating that the people's food and drink, as well as their language and attire, are like those in mid-India. Thus, they belonged to the Indian race. He further describes the religion of Buddha as very flourishing and mentions that Sakya visited this country to convert a wicked Naga. The pilgrim also says that the Nagas of the Tsung-ling mountains (Hindu Kush), when evil-disposed of, spit poison, winds, rain, and snow, etc.; he notes, too, that in Udyana, a stranger was entertained for three days and was then " requested to find a place for himself." This is a Rajput tradition that Quintus Curtius mentions in his account of Taxiles entertaining Alexander, and which is still in use today.

Sung Yun, another pilgrim, entered Udyana about A.D. 518 by way of the Kashkara (Chitral) valley. He records that the king of the country was then a Buddhist who observed a vegetable diet and that Buddhism was flourishing. This pilgrim mentions a regular system of irrigation from the rivers, which indicates a considerable degree of civilization. Additionally, he describes a Naga temple that had fifty or more priests serving it and claims that the king offers the Naga gold jewels and other priceless sacrifices. Sung Yun mentioned that the neighboring kingdom of Gandhara had been destroyed two generations before by Yetha invaders, but these had evidently retired from the country before his visit. A third Chinese pilgrim, Hiouen Tsiang, visited these countries about A.D. 630. He arrived by way of Bamian, Kapisa, and the Kabul Valley, from which he traveled through Gandhara and Udyana to Takshasila. This pilgrim, like the others, found Buddhism existing in all of these countries, side by side with the worship of the Devas and the Nagas, which were everywhere popular deities. Describing Kapisa., or Kabul, Hiouen Tsiang says that this country is 4000 Ii or so in the circuit, that on the north, it adjoins the snowy mountains, and that on three sides, it borders upon the Hindu Kush. The people he describes as "cruel and fierce." He says, "The king is a Kshatriya by caste. The king was a Buddhist, and there were roughly 1,000 viharas, 6,000 priests, ten temples dedicated to Devas, a thousand heretics, naked ascetics, and some who "covered themselves with ashes, and others who made chaplets of bones, which they wore as crowns upon their heads.

These are all well-known forms of Hindu asceticism." Two hundred miles from the royal city was a great snowy mountain, upon which was a lake. The king is cunning, brave, and determined, and he has subjugated the neighboring countries, about ten of which he rules." Here, the Naga demi-god of the lake granted the wishes of whoever prayed for good weather or asked for rain. There once was an Arhat from Gandharaj who accepted the religious offerings from the Naga monarch. In other words, he served as his priest. According to the pilgrim, a previous Naga raja of this lake was killed by another Naga, who took hold of his belongings and unleashed severe storms. The Naga demolished a stupa and vihara constructed by Kanishka Raja six times. When Kanishka finally gathered his army, he intended to destroy the serpent chief, but he eventually submitted. In Lamghan, under Kapisa's rule, there were numerous Deva temples and roughly ten sungharamas with a small following. Naga Gopala's dwelling (shrine) was in a large cavern. Several Buddha relics, including a skull, a bone, and an eyeball, were found in the nearby town of Hidda. The people who once resided in Gandhara, which was under the control of an officer from Kapisa, are the ancestors of the king of Kabul and many other nearby nations. In the city of Udabhandapura, also called Waihand, which Cunningham and Stein both mentioned was one of the centers of the Hindu Shahiya dynasty, this king hosted Hiouen Tsiang during his journey back to China. The king marched the pilgrims to Kabul via Lamghan. This demonstrates once more that the Kshatriya king of Kabul was a Sahis of the Gandharan Kator or Pala dynasty. The pilgrim reports that while some towns and villages were abandoned, others were thriving.

Snake deity, Southern India

There were numerous Deva temples as well as sungharamas and stupas, some of which were in ruins. Men from all over India are said to have traveled to the temple of Bhima Devi to fulfill their vows. Sung Yun claims that the Yetha destroyed this nation two generations prior in A.D. 520. Evidently, the Hindu rajas had regained control. The pilgrims who came before Hiouen Tsiang had written about Udyana, which was their next destination. He discovered that although there was still a lot of respect for the Buddha's law, Buddhism was not as strong as it once was. The pilgrim visited the Naga Apalala fountain, the source of the Swat River, and observed the Devas' temples, where the Naga demigods continued to rule the elements and oversee the lakes and fountains. He also went to the stupa that Uttara Sena, the Sakya king of Udyana, had built over the Buddha's relics. Hiouen Tsiang tells the tale of the Uttara Sena and how his union with the Naga raja's daughter helped him win the kingdom. In addition, he claims that the hoods of a nine-headed Naga materialized over the princess's head. Hiouen Tsiang traveled to Tak-Shasila, which he claims was once under Kabul rule but is now a tributary of Kash-Mir, after stopping by Darel and a few other nearby valleys. Buddhism also doesn't seem to be as strong here as it once was.

Though numerous, the sungharamas were abandoned and in ruins. Of course, the Buddhist pilgrims' attention was primarily focused on Buddhist monuments and institutions, but their accounts of the countries they passed through were fascinating. The pilgrim tells us that the people of Takshasila wished for rain or fine weather, and they went with Buddhist priests to the tank of the Naga raja Elapatra, where, after praying, they immediately obtained their desires. This source tells us that Hindus survived into the seventh century of our era in the kingdoms south of the Hindu Kush, from Kabul to the Indus. We also discover that at that time, Buddhism coexisted with the worship of the Devas, Nagas, and Brahmanical gods throughout these nations. We also find that the Naga demigods were widely worshipped as popular deities ruling the elements and revered for their sacred fountains, lakes, and streams. As a result, it seems certain that Naga worshippers continued to reside in the area surrounding Kabul and between Kabul and Kashmir until the early Mohammedan invasions, which took place in the middle of the seventh century, just a few years after the visit of Hiouen Tsang. Furthermore, there is little doubt that these people descended from Ahi's or Azi's serpent race, who resisted the advancing Aryas in this very tract.

The paramount rulers of this people were the Kator Sahis of Kabul and Gandhara. This dynasty belonged to Rajpal, Anandpal, Trilochanpal, and other less well-known chiefs who, as Abu Rihan undoubtedly mentions in a passage that has generated much debate, resisted the Mohammedan invaders for so long and with such tenacity. Kabul must have experienced many vicissitudes during the turbulent times that followed Alexander's overthrow of the great Persian empire. There is no doubt that for a while, foreign powers ruled it. But most people must have continued to be Hindu. It's also likely that the indigenous leaders held onto a semblance of power and made their presence known when the chance presented itself. Chinese Buddhist chronicles state that Guna Yarman, the grandson of a former Kabul monarch, traveled to China via Ceylon and Java in the year A.D. 424 and traveled to the capital of the Sung dynasty. Based on this, it appears that Hindμ kings ruled Kabul for over two centuries, approximately in the year A.D. The first time the Islamic armies captured Kabul was during the reign of Muawiya, around the middle of the seventh century, about twenty years after Hiouen Tsiang's visit.

Kabul was the coronation city of the Pala dynasty, and a king was properly inaugurated once he had been installed there. He discovered a Kshatriya king on the throne in 63. The king, referred to by the historians of the Mussulmans as Kabul Shah (the Sahi of Kabul), made an appeal to the Hind warriors, who came to his aid in such large numbers that the invaders were forced out of Kabul and the surrounding region, all the way to Bost. It is unclear if this Kabul king was the same one who hosted the Chinese pilgrim, but he too had to be a Kshatriya or the Hind warriors would not have paid much attention to his plea. The Mohammedan armies returned with ample reinforcements, and Kabul was retaken once more after the king consented to pay tribute. Following the Mohammedan occupation of Kabul, the chiefs of the Hindu Shahi dynasty lived primarily in Udakabhanda. They controlled almost all of Punjab and remained strong. They ruled from Kashmir to Multan and from Sarhind to Lamghan until Mahmud finally toppled them in the eleventh century. Over nearly four centuries, the Kater Sahis and the Muslim invaders fought each other almost nonstop. Albiruni is said to have found the Kabul Sahis' genealogy written on silk in the fort of Nagarkot or Kangra. The Sabi kings were so powerful that in the Rajatarangini, the glory of the Sabi is compared to that of the Sun among the stars of heaven.

All the prominent chiefs of Northern India sent their contingents to support the Sahis against the Mohammedan invaders. This renowned fortress served as the stronghold of the Trigarta, or Jalandhara, family, with whom the Sahis intermarried. Even though they are now Mohammedans, some of the tribes south of the Hindu Kush still go by the names Manu gave them. Wilson pointed out that the Kafir tribe of Kamoj was most likely speaking for the Kambajas. Of these chiefs, the Chohan Raja of Ajmir is specifically said to have been related to the Sahi Jaipal. Furthermore, it is unlikely that some of the country's invaders drove a remnant of the Kambojas into the mountains. In actuality, according to popular belief, the Kamoj were expelled from Kandahar. (Gandhara). Manu describes the Shinas or Chinas and their neighbors, the Daradas, as fallen Kshatriyas. The Kambojas and Gandharas appear to have been neighbors at the time described in the Mahabharata. The Shinas, who are arguably the Chinas of the Mahabharata and are still found in some places still called China, are also mentioned in the Mahabharata in relation to the Kambojas, Kasmiras, and other northern tribes! are, like most of their neighbors, of the solar race.

Biddulph cited a song by Shina that goes like this: "The forest serpent, Suri Mohammad Khan, rouses himself. Beyond Shahrot, he will brandish his sword, the forest serpent of the race of Mallika. "Here, the chief bears a Mohammedan name, but he is declared to be of the serpent race, while Suri is the Shina name for the Sun. The Shinas, though now Mohammedans, retain many of their ancient customs, which are much the same as those existing in the Himalayas. The cedar and the juniper are held sacred and are believed to afford protection from evil spirits. The seed corn, before sowing, is purified in the smoke of the cedar. The Daradas still inhabit the left bank of the Indus. They are frequently alluded to in the Rajatarangini, and they held then, as they do now, the country between the north-western boundary of Kashmir and the Indus. The Darada chiefs, like those of Kator, were called Sahi or Shahi. The Daradas, although described in the Mahabharata as " good and well-born Kshatriyas," had evidently, like their neighbors, come but little under Brahmanical influence, even down to the time of their conversion to Islam. Amongst the tribes of the Hindu Kush, springs are still supposed to cause storms if any impurity is thrown into them, owing to the resentment of the Sun or of the Naga, to whichever they may be sacred. Shahi Jaipal is said to have submitted to Amir Subuktigin because of a snowstorm created in this manner. The rulers of Hunza and Nagar, who are now Mohammedans, are still thought to have authority over the elements, just as the Ahi of the Rig Veda and other Naga rajas did.

It appears likely that Takha, or Katha, was not a tribal name but rather a term given to several tribes. The Takhas are not listed among the people fighting in the Mahabharata, either by that name or any of its modern variations nor are any of these referred to as Nagas. However, Hemachandra notes that people who go by the names Bahikas, Bahlikas, or Vahlikas are also known as Takhas. The Bahikas, also known as Bahlikas, were allies of the Kauravas during the Great War. They were obviously very influential individuals with a lot of power in the nation. The regions they inhabited lined up with the dominions of the Naga Rajas and later with the Takhia kingdom. It is unclear where the term Bahika, also known as Bahlika, originated, but it was clearly not a tribal name. Some have assumed that these individuals must be Balkan invaders. But even in that far-off era, they were not recent invaders.

Anuradhapura Snake Shrine in Sri Lanka

According to Kern, the Atharva Veda does mention them, whereas the Rig Veda does not, and Panini refers to them as people who settled in India and spoke a dialect that was somewhat distinct from that of their neighbors. The messengers Dasarath sent to fetch Bharata from Kckaya, traveling through Panchala, Kurujangala, and the heart of Vahlika, serve as proof that they arrived in Punjab before the Ramayana. Vahlika, also spelled Bhalika, seems to have been a collective term for several Solar Race tribes or clans that were comparatively close to one another.

These are mentioned with reference to the Prasthalas, Madras, Gandharas, Arattas, Khasas, Vasatis, Sindhus, and Sauviras; they are most likely included with them as well. According to reports, the Bahlikas reside in the regions of Panjab, Sind, and Rajputana that the rivers Satadru (Sutlej), Vipasa (Beas), Iravati (Ravi), Chandra-bigha (Chinab), Vitasta (Jhelum), and Sindhu (Indus) traverse. The Sutlej used to flow much further south than it does now. The hundred kings of Bahlika, who ruled over these people, were many chiefs. During the great war, Salya, a grandson of Somadatta, or Vahlika, a Bharata chief, was the foremost ruler of the Bahlikas. Vahlika had succeeded to the throne of the Bhalika raja, his maternal grandfather. The Bahlikas, or Takhas, were "good and well-born Kshatriyas" who intermarried with the Bharatas, but they were obviously unregenerate and had not yet embraced Aryan customs. Salya and other Bhalika chiefs were present at Rukmini's swayambara, or choice of a husband. The Madras were one of the most significant tribes of the Bahlikas, as we will see from the practices attributed to them shortly. Sakala was a Madras city and the capital of the Bahlika Raja.

The Madras are described as Danavas in the Katha Sarit Sagara, and all these tribes were undoubtedly descended from the Asuras. The Kurus and Panchalas, who had clearly been influenced by Brahmanical law, are described as "conversant with the truths of religion," but this is not the case for the Madrakas and the other people of the "Five Rivers." Several of the customs attributed to the Bahlikas were undoubtedly in conflict with the laws established by Brahmanical law-givers. The Madras are said to have had Kshatriya priests, which was one of their greatest transgressions. Some of the irregularities may have been exaggerated, but many of them persist among these people's descendants. Notably, this supports other verses that indicate the Bahlikas were Kshatriyas and did not belong to any outside barbarian tribe or servile caste. These people are described as eating out of wooden and earthen vessels and drinking the milk of sheep and camels, which some of them still do. However, we find that they had not adopted a fixed caste system and that there were Brahmans and Kshatriyas in the same family. It is also said that all the tribes drank strong liquors and that the Jartika clan of the Bahikas and the Sakala people ate beef with garlic. It is believed that a location for storing alcoholic beverages and a cattle slaughterhouse mark the entrance to the homes of the Vahika chiefs.

The women are also accused of engaging in other inappropriate behavior, including drinking and dancing in public. At Dwaraka and Indraprastha, however, some of these orthodox Yadavas and Bharatas adopted some of these heterodox customs. We learn that during festivals, the Yadava women in Dwaraka danced and sang and that the rishi Narada entertained them with music on the vina. Once more, the ladies—among whom were Draupadi and Subhadra—drank wine during the celebration that Krishna and Arjuna attended with their families and friends by the Yamuna. Some of them even started dancing and singing, and some even started to walk unsteadily. All of these practices that were against Hindu law-giver regulations are evidence that Asura customs likely predate Brahmanical influence. It is still common in the Himalayas for Kshatriyas to serve as priests at both Deva and Naga temples. The plains Rajputs, however, are accustomed to this custom. According to Colonel Tod, the Ranas of Mewar take precedence over the priest and carry out the rituals when they visit the Siva temple. There are other temples where this is done.

The Ras Mala tells us that the Rana himself makes sacrifices, fans the idol with a chaori, and accepts the offerings at the shrine of Amba Bhowanie Mata, the tutelary deity of the Pramaras. There are also some old Vishnu temples at Rajim, Kosala; the Bais Rajputs own one of the oldest of these, the pujaris. Here, orthodox Hindus continue to practice the Asura custom of Kshatriya priests, which the Bahlikas first adopted. It is said that the Asura king was granted six privileges when Vishnu, in the Dwarf Avatara, took away the dominions of the Daitya chief Bali, except for Patala. Two of these were that he should offer something without a priest and that he should make a sraddha without Brahmans. This seems to indicate that the Aryas and the Asuras had a religious agreement, or the "Concordat." Many Kshatriya tribes were still unregenerate during the period that the Mahabharata describes. It is said that all the Arattas, Khasas, Vasatis, Sindhus, and Sauviras were equally evil and that some of the other gods weren't much better. Against Brahmanical precepts, the Madras received a price for their daughters' marriages. However, it turns out that when Bhishma, the chief of the Bharata, tried to get Madri to marry Pandu, he followed this custom.

And he gave "much gold," in addition to jewels, to the princess's older brother Salya, who gave her away as the family's head. As we've just seen, one of the evil customs associated with the Bahlikas is the use of earthen and wooden vessels to hold food. The descendants of these people still harbor animosity toward the brass vessels that all orthodox Hindus use and prefer wooden or earthenware ones in their place. Earthen vessels are commonly observed in the Punjab plains due to the limited availability of suitable wood. When a stranger uses them, these frequently break. Wooden vessels are fairly common in areas with an abundance of timber, such as the Hindu Kush or the Himalayas. These are usually of an oval shape and deeply bellied," as described in the Mahabharata. Bahlikas, or Takhas. Sakala, the capital of Salya, the Bahlika Raja, was a Takha city. Sakala was on the Apaga, or Aik River, and was the Sangala of the Greeks. This city was, at the time of Alexander's invasion in the fourth century B.C., a fortress of the Kathias, who, as already noted, were included amongst the Takhas. Sakala was in ruins when the Chinese pilgrim Hiouen Tsiang visited it in the seventh century A.D., but the surrounding region was still a part of the Takha, or Takhia, kingdom. And it did so at the time of the Arab invasion of Sind in the eighth century.

Moreover, the Kathia tribe still holds land around their ancient stronghold to this day. The descendants of the Bahikas, or Bahlikas, who still live amongst "the forests of Pilu and Karira" on the banks of the "Five Rivers," as their forefathers did in the time of Salya, are now Mohammedans. Still, they retain many of the customs ascribed to their ancestors in the Mahabharata and by the chroniclers of Alexander's invasion. They are divided into numerous tribes or clans, of which the Kathias are among the most powerful. These people, notwithstanding their conventional version of Islam, are proud of their Kshatriya descent, but, of course, they no longer worship the Naga demi-gods. They still retain the handsome features and fine physique with which the Greeks were so impressed. Their sacred groves, once the abodes of the gods, are still religiously preserved. In them, no tree is felled, nor is even a branch broken. These are now used as burial places, and bodies are brought from long distances to be laid in them.

Women, among these people, are still allowed much more freedom than is generally the case in India. They are not secluded; the daughters, like the heroines of the Mahabharata, are married as grown-up young women and infant marriage is unknown. When a boy reaches manhood, the father ties a sparse pagri, or turban (the fillet of Strabo), around his son's head, and the men allow their hair and beards to grow, as the Greek writers described. Until recently, this ceremony was not performed until the youth had shown his prowess by killing an enemy or by lifting cattle. I once heard a village patriarch acknowledge that this was the custom of his people, and he added, regretfully, that it had become very difficult to carry it out. His grandson, who was standing by and wearing nothing but a hat, said this.

Ornate carving of a Naga, Hindu snake god, Banteay Srei Temple, Cambodia.

No doubt, the youth won his turban not long after. In the early days of British rule, in the Panjab, almost the only crimes amongst these people were cattle stealing and the affrays resulting from it. These latter often ended fatally for some of those engaged. In most villages were men called "Kojis," who could follow the footmarks of men or cattle for almost any distance and whose services were in frequent demand.

When stolen cattle were traced to a village, and there seemed no hope of evading punishment, it was not uncommon for some of the older men to give themselves up in order to screen the young ones who were the real criminals. This was probably a survival from the good old days when the necessity of keeping up the fighting strength of the tribe was urgent. These people are, with their relatives, the Sikhs, the finest race in India. Some of the Kathias and other descendants of the Bahlikas, as well as branches of other Kshatriya tribes, are called Jats. The origin of the Jats has been much discussed. Some authorities have considered them to be descendants of invading Scythian hordes. There can be no doubt, however, that, whatever its origin, the term Jat has long been applied to the descendants of those Kshatriyas who clung to their ancient customs and to branches of Rajput tribes who, in consequence of irregular practices, have been cast off by their more orthodox relatives. Nearly every Rajput tribe has Jat branches.

Thus, the Bhattis of Jaisalmer, who are Rajputs of the Lunar line, apply the term Jat in their genealogical lists to those of their own tribe who have married beneath them, have adopted unorthodox practices, or have become converts to Islam. In the Panjab, the Kathias, Khurrals, Johyas, and other tribes are each divided into Rajputs and Jats. In other parts of India, the same conditions occur, and Jat clans are found to be of undoubted Rajput descent. Sir H. Elliot mentions a tribe of Jats who are descended, in the direct line, from Rai Pirthiraj Chohan.' M. Vivien de St. Martin has noted that the name Jartika, given to one branch of the Bahlikas in the Mahabharata, is a Sanskrit translation of the word Jat. This shows that there were Jats on the banks of the "Five Rivers at the time of the great war and goes far to confirm the view that Rajputs and Jats are of the same stock, the difference between them being one of orthodoxy only.The Kathis, or Kathias, of Kathiawar, is a branch of the Kathias 'of the Panjab. Tribal customs state that this branch of the Kathias originated in what is now known as Bikanir and then relocated to the Indus Valley. They continued and reached Kathiawar in the thirteenth century. Some of the tribe's wanderers appear to have made their way to the Ganges valley, while other groups of people went in different directions. This migration most likely resulted from the then-significant alteration in Sutlej's course. At that point, the river abandoned its old course, which is now known as the "Hakra," and joined the Beas. Naturally, this shift left a sizable area of previously fertile land—complete with numerous significant towns and countless villages—without water. According to tradition, thousands of men and cattle perished from starvation and drought as a result, with the majority of survivors seeking safety in the Indus Valley. The region along the former Sutlej bed is now a desert, but the Kathias of Kathiawar, who are essentially orthodox Hindus, still honor the Sun and the serpent. There are many shrines dedicated to Vasuki and other Naga demi-gods; Colonel Tod informs us that these are Takshaka people. In certifying significant legal documents, they invoke "the holy sun." The Kathi assert that they supported the Kauravas during the epic battle of the Mahabharata. They were a division of the Kathias, as was previously stated. According to an inscription from Ramchandrapur, close to Bundi in Rajputana, which Colonel Tod cited, the warrior Takhya, who fashioned the skull garland around Mahadeo's neck, belonged to the Catti (Kathi) tribe. The Vahlas, also known as the Bahlas or the Bahilkas, are believed to have been lords of Arore in the Indus Valley.

The bards referred to their chiefs as "Tatha Multan ka rai," or kings of Tatha and Multan. These people are closely associated with the Kuthis and appear to be of the same stock. Balas and Kathis are presumably branches of the same people; the name Vahla, or Bala, recalls that of the great Asura Bali of Patala, who likewise ruled from the mouth of the Indus to Multan. This title is also given to the Kathis ", and the term Kathiani bai, or Kathia lady, is sometimes applied to ladies of the Vahla family. We know from the Mahabharata that the Bahlikas, or Takhas, occupied the country on the banks of the Indus at a very early period. The Balika rai, who held the same tract of country in ancient times, may have been descendants of the Daityn king. An inscription from approximately the year A.D. can be found on an iron pillar located in Delhi. According to 4I5, Chandra Gupta II erected it as a monument to his victory over the Sindhuan Vahlikas. Thus, Bahlikn chiefs continued to rule the Indus Valley until the first time this pillar was built. Furthermore, as we have already seen, the descendants of the Naga Rajas continued to rule in the Indus Valley until Hiouen Tsiang's visit in the seventh century, when Multan and the surrounding region became a part of the kingdom of Takhya. It appears that more than one of these Kshatriya tribes was known by multiple names. As we have seen, the epic poems did not call the Takhas or Kathas by those names; instead, they were called Bahlikas. Some of these were simply insults that their bards or neighbors threw at them, while others might have come from branches off the main stem. The Mahabharata made no mention of the strong Puars, also known as Pramaras, under either of these titles. The Puars' dominions stretched from the Indus to the Jumna and even farther.

Naga (seven-headed snake) statue at Angkor Wat, Cambodia.

The Indian rajas, referred to as Phur by Ferishta and other historians and as Porus by the chroniclers of Alexander's expedition, most likely belonged to this powerful tribe. The historians of Alexander claimed that two of the chiefs who went by the name Porus were related to one another. Therefore, this was a tribal or racial name rather than a personal one. Ferishta also states that Phur was the Raja of Kather, or Kamaon, which the bards claim was a part of the Puar dominions. Mr. The Vishnu Purana states that Vidmisara, or Bimbisaro, was a great-great-grandson of Sisunaga, King of Magadha. The great Asoka, grandson of Chandragupta Marya, seems to have worshipped the Naga even after he converted to Buddhism. We are told that when Asoka heard that Mahakilo, the Naga raja, had seen the last four Buddhas, he sent for him, or rather for the living serpent, which represented him. Grierson has recently brought attention to the close relationship between the dialects of the Rajas and those of the Himalayan dialects. When the Naga arrived, Asoka placed him" on the royal throne, under the white canopy of dominion' and, making many flower offerings requested to be shown the appearance of Buddha. This request, we are told, was granted.

In the time of Asoka, Naga rajas were numerous and powerful. We find that when this king, wishing to divide the relics of Buddha amongst the new stupas that he had built, went with an army to remove the relics from the old stupa at Ramagrama, the Nagas refused to allow him to do so. And Asoka, powerful as he was, did not persist. This stupa is said to have been carried away by the river afterward. However, the Nga people saved the artifacts and transported them to Majerika on the Kistna River, where the Naga Raja, who ruled that nation, constructed a magnificent stupa over them. In the Vishnu Purana, it is said that nine Nagas will reign in Padmavati, Kantipura, and Mathara. Sir A. Cunningham has demonstrated that these serpent chiefs, whose names he gives from their coins, held the majority of the country between the Jumna and the Narbada and that they ruled as independent princes during the first two centuries of the Christian era. According to the inscription on the Allahabad pillar, most of the Naga chiefs of any importance who remained in his time seem to have been overthrown by Samudra Gupta. The Naga people disappeared from history at about the time of the downfall of the Buddhist religion. The Brahmanic revival was fatal to both, and the Nagas, like the Buddhists, were induced or compelled to adopt orthodox Hinduism.

A small statue, the temple of the serpent in Gokarna, India

5. DRAVIDIANS

The Dravidians are typically credited with founding the first civilization in southern India. Many authorities believe this individual originated in northern India. The Aryas who drove them from their homes. Here, as elsewhere, it is assumed that the Aryas were conquerors who reduced the Asuras to slavery. Dr. Caldwell, a very eminent authority, asks: "Were the Dravidians identical with the Dasyus, by whom the progress of the Aryans was disputed, and who were finally subdued and incorporated with the Aryan race as their serfs and dependents?" But this was different, as these pages have already demonstrated. The two people were fused together. Furthermore, we have seen that the Asuras did not submit to the Aryas, nor did they become their serfs or dependents, but instead progressively assimilated into Aryan customs, independent of what happened to the native people. According to Dr. Caldwell himself, "Neither any Sanskrit authority nor any Dravidian tradition recognizes the subjugation of the Dravidians by the Aryans nor the expulsion of the southern Dravidians from northern India," the Asuras or Dravidians had, despite this, established colonies in the south, as we have seen in the case of the Nagas, sons of Kadru and Lavana before them. There can be little doubt that Asura colonists were the ones who founded the Dravidian kingdoms, as some of these colonies were in the exact locations that those kingdoms now occupy.

Some of these colonies may have existed before the Aryas arrived in India; expeditions sent from Patala and other ports founded these Dravidian colonies, some by land and some by sea. Old legends mention conflicts between the Hindu colonists of later times, who were allegedly under Parasu Rama's leadership, and the Nagas from Patala, who they discovered to oversee the nation. Additionally, inscriptions from the tenth and eleventh centuries demonstrate that several chiefs in southwest India asserted direct descent from the Naga rajas of Patala, claiming to have been born into the race of the Nagas, to have carried the Naga dhwaja, or serpent banner, and to have possessed the hereditary title of "supreme lord of Rhogavati." Iagarakhanda, or the land of the Naga people, was the name given to a portion of Kanara in inscriptions. These people established the first settlements in Ceylon, but later, invaders from India drove them out in part. As we've already seen, the legendary Ruvana, the enemy of Rama, was a Patiala-born Naga chief whose kingdom was probably one of the Naga colonies. Buddhist authorities state that powerful serpent race chiefs lived in Ceylon before the Buddha. Although their colonies were numerous and extensive, their docs do not appear to have been any general migration southwards of the Asura people.

They never abandoned their possessions in northern India, and in the new territories, even where dynasties were established, the greater part of the population seems to have remained of the Nishada or aboriginal race, as in the kingdom of the Naga Raja Dhumavarna, which has already been referred to. The invaders, however, appear to have been able, owing to their superior civilization, to impress upon the rude aboriginal people their social customs, religion, and language. The Dravidian colonists, too, seem to have intermixed to some extent with the surrounding population, which would be sufficient to account for the caste of Sudra having been assigned to their descendants. This also explains the existence of Dravidian dialects and customs amongst people., such as the Gonds and others, whose appearance would indicate aboriginal descent rather than any relationship to the inhabitants of the Indus Valley or Panjab.

The worship of the Brahmanical deities was introduced in the south long after the time of these early colonists when the Saiva and Vaishnava forms of Hinduism had become established in northern India, and the Devas and Asuras had united into one people. The widespread veneration of the Naga demi-gods, the abundance of unorthodox deities with their equally unorthodox rites, and the numerous customs that Brahmanical lawgivers do not recognize are indications that the people have nevertheless retained much of their ancient religion and way of life. People who are ostensibly descended from the Nagas or Asuras still practice most of these religions and many of these customs in various parts of northern India. The worship of the Naga, or hooded serpent, is common amongst the Dravidian people of the south. Rudely sculptured representations of the Serpent or of the Naga demi-gods, to which offerings are regularly made, are to be found under nearly every large tree. Here, as in the north, it is the Naga or Cobra, here called Chera, which is held sacred, is a welcome visitor, and must not be killed. Here, too, as in the Himalayas, it is as the totem of their Naga forefathers that the Nulla Paumbhu, or good snake, is venerated.

Serpent temple Thiruvananthapuram Kerala India, Snake idol

To the Naga demi-gods, as ancestors, divine honors are paid. Amongst these ancestors of the Dravidians are the same Nuga rajas who are worshipped, also as ancestors, by the descendants of the Asuras in the north of India. As already mentioned, the offerings made to living serpents, as well as to their sculptured representatives, consist of milk, flour, fruit, and grain, which are not the usual food of snakes but are the food of men. Flowers and lights are also offered to ancestors. We find, too, that should a cobra be killed, it is burned as if it were a human body, and it is even provided with a winding sheet. The Dravidians typically worship the Naga demi-gods in Kavus, or groves shielded from axes and spades, much like the sacred groves close to so many villages in Punjab. Sometimes, these groves are very extensive, and many of the temples are richly endowed; one of these, Kavus, occupies the southwest corner of the enclosure around each Nair house. The Naga Raja temple at Nagercoil is among the most well-known in all of Travancore.

A family who owns a Naga Kavu close to Travancore claims that their ancestors were among the Nagas spared when the Confederate tribes under the leadership of Krishna and Arjuna burned the Khandava forest in Punjab. The members of this household are temple priests; in addition to the groves and temples sacred to the Naga demigods, there are, as in northern India, groves and temples dedicated to Devas. The eldest female member of the family, who must maintain celibacy, carries the image of the serpent god in the solemn procession that circles the shrine during the festivals held in honor of the Nuga raja. Every male member of this household bears the name of Vasuki, the raja of Patala and the deified hero of the Naga people of northern India. All these nonorthodox shrines use the local Dravidian dialect for their services; in the Brahmanical temples, however, Sanskrit is used for the worship of the orthodox deities.

There are other deities as well, some of whom are likely of Aboriginal descent and some of whom are female. It is impossible not to recognize in the so-called demon worship of the Dravidian people, as described by Dr. Caldwell and others, a more debased form of the ancestor worship of northern India and other countries; some of the rituals, and perhaps some of the deities, may have been borrowed from the aboriginal tribes, but the main features of the ceremonial are identical to the forms used in the worship of the Devas and Nagas in the Himalayas; some of the deities, too, are the same; sacred groves, temples owned by the villagers and not under the control of Brahmins, non-Brahminic priests, inspired prophets, religious dances, circumambulating temples, flagellation, and the rituals associated with raising the Dhwaja, or god's flag, are all things that both the old but less rigorous Hi. An additional connection between the northern descendants of Asuras and the southern Dravidians is the custom of having dancing girls affixed to temples. These are the Apsaras, or celestial nymphs, whose allures, as the epic poems and Puranas tell us, so frequently tampered with the penance of holy men in the past. From the Mahabharata, we learn that the princes of Kshatriya from northern India often had marriages with the ruling Dravidian families; thus, two of the chiefs of the early Bharata, Akrodhana and Tangsu, married princesses of Kalinga and Arjuna married the daughter of the Pandya king. We have it, however, on the authority of Mann that the Dravidas were of Kshatriya origin. He mentions them among those Kshatriyas who had sunk to the condition of Suclras through the omission of sacred rites and the neglect of Brfihmans. This, of course, refers only to the ruling families and military castes. Later, among other instances, Ranaditya, raja of Kashmir, married the daughter of Ratiscna, raja of Chola. This, according to the Rajatarangini, is about A.D. 300.

We also learn from Manu that the Dravidas are descended from Vratya Kshatriyas, just like the Mallas, Lichavis, Kasas, and others. While Kshatriyas were Solar race tribes that worshipped Nagas, the Mallas, Lichavis, and Kasas continued to follow the traditions and religion of their Asnra ancestors, and it seems that Manu saw the Dravidas as the same. In the Mahabharata, Karna compares the Karashkaras, Mahishakas, Kalingas, Keralas, Karkotakas, and Virakas to the Bahikas of northern India during his dispute with Salya. However, there is additional proof that the serpent-worshippers in southern India were closely connected to those in northern India. The Dravidian people have been divided, from ancient times, into Cheras, Cobas, and Pandyas. Chera, or Sera (in old Tamil Sarai), is the Dravidian equivalent for Naga; Chera-mandala, therefore, has the same meaning as Naga-mandala, Naga-dwipa, or the Naga country. This points distinctly to the Asura origin of the Dravidians of the south. But in addition to this, there still exists, widely spread over the Ganges valley, a people who call themselves Cherus or Seoris and who claim descent from the serpent gods.

The Naga tribes first settled the Ganges valley, which, as we have already seen, was once home to the Cherus, an extremely ancient race. The Cherus appear to have been gradually ousted from their lands during the troubled times of the Mohammedan invasions, and they are now poor and almost landless. There can be little doubt that these people are the relatives of the Dravidian Cheras. The Cherus have severe peculiar customs, and among them is one that seems to connect them with the Lichavis as well as with the Newars of Nepal. This is the election of a raja for every five or six houses and his investiture, in due form, with the tilak, or royal frontal mark. Both Lichavis and Newars had many customs in common with the Dravidians of the south. Each venerated the Serpent, Karkotaka Naga, being to Nepal what Nila Naga was to Kashmir.

Relief Carving on Stone Plate, Madhukeshwara Temple, India

The marriage relationships between Newars and Lichavis bore striking similarities to Tamil marriages, even indicating a shared ancestor. In short, a recent Dravidian writer, Mr. Balkrishna Nair, says that his people "appear to be, in nearly every particular, the kinsfolk of the Newars." Property among the Newars descended in the female line, as did among the Arattas, Bahikas, or Takhas of the Panjab, whose sisters' sons, and not their own, were their heirs. This is still a Dravidian custom. According to an inscription that Colonel Tod discovered at Kanswah close to the river Chambal, the raja of Takhya was named Salindra and was "of the race of Sarya, a tribe renowned among the tribes of the mighty." Despite all of this, however, there are still other connections that bind the Naga people of the south and north of India. The Naga people of Takhya were also called Sarya, and this was definitely the Takhya or Takha kingdom of the Panjab, which Hiouen Tsiang visited and about which we have already spoken. Once more, the Naga demi-gods are the principal deities worshipped in the Sarraj district, which is located in the outer Himalayas between the Sutlej and Beas valleys.

There is another Seoraj in the upper Chinab valley where Naga worshippers reside. Apparently, therefore, the Saryas of Takhya, the Sarraj people of the Sutlej valley, the Seoris or Cherus of the Ganges valley, and the Cheras, Seras, or Keralas of southern India are but different branches of the same Naga-worshipping people. The name Saraj, or Seoraj, appears to be the same as the Sarya of Colonel Tod's inscription and as Seori, which is the alternative name of the Cherus of the Ganges valley. It is also identical to Sarai, which, as we have already seen, is the old Tamil name for the Chera or Naga. Kira, or Kiri, means a serpent in some Himalayan dialects; Varaha Mihira mentions the Kiras, which are on a copper plate published by Prof. Kielhorn; this name, from which the term Kirata was derived and is so frequently applied to people of the Himalayas, is found in the Rajatarangini. Kiragrama is the name of the place mentioned in an inscription at the Baijnath temple in the Kangra Valley; this would mean the village of serpents in the local dialect. The term Kira is thus equivalent to Naga, and it can scarcely be doubted that the serpent worshipping Kiras of the Himalayas were closely related to the Dravidian Keras, Cheras, or Keralas of the south. The Naga is still a popular deity at Baijnath and throughout the neighboring country. These people, whose designation is thus apparently the same, are all of the Solar race; they all revered the hooded Serpent, and they all worshipped the Naga demi-gods as ancestors. Name similarity is only sometimes to be trusted, but here we have something more.

Based on the previous information, it is fairly likely that the Dravidians in southern India were descended from the same ancestors as the northern Nagas or Asuras. The only matter left to resolve is speech; the language of the southern Dravidians is not the same as that of the northern Indians, but those who would protest linguistically against the Dravidians and Nagas having a common ancestor should remember that the Asuras, who seem to be of Turanian descent, would speak Turanian. While later authorities have also considered these dialects to have Scythian affinities, Sir W. Jones long ago identified a "Tartarian or Chaldee element" in the regional vernaculars of northern India. Dr. Caldwell goes a step further, stating: "Seeing that the northern vernaculars possess, with the. It seems more accurate to describe those languages as having a Scythian basis with a significant and nearly overwhelming Sanskrit addition rather than a Sanskrit basis with a minor admixture of a Scythian element because of the Sanskrit words, which have a grammatical structure that mostly appears to be Scythian." Based on what we have seen so far, there can be little doubt that the corrupting influences that gave rise to the various Prakrits originated primarily from the language of the Asuras; the linguistic changes that resulted from the gradual fusion of the Aryas and Dasyus were what made so many grammarians necessary.

It should also be remembered that the Prakrits were formed at a later period when the two peoples had become welded together; therefore, it is expected that the Prakrits should have a closer affinity with Sanskrit than the Dravidian languages of southern India and that the latter should retain a more intimate connection than the Prakrits with Scythian or Turanian tongues. The Asuras appear to have sent out their earlier colonies prior to their fusion with the Aryas, and at that time, their language could have come under the influence of Sanskrit but little. The old Sanskrit grammarians considered the language of the Dravidian countries to relate to the vernaculars of northern India and that, in their opinion, it was especially related to the speech of those people who, as we have seen, were apparently descendants of the Asura tribes. Thus, in the "Shadbasha Chandrika," Lakshmidhara says that the Paisachi language is spoken in the Paisachi countries of Pandya, Kekaya, Vahlika, Sahya, Nepala, Kuntala, Sudesha, Bhota, Gandhara, Haiva, and Kanojana, and that these are the Paisachi countries. Of all the vernacular dialects, the Paisachi is said to have contained the smallest infusion of Sanscrit. The fact that the Asuras originally spoke a language that differed from that of the Aryas seems evident. Professor Muir quotes several passages from the Rig Veda in which the word "mridavach" refers to the Asuras' speech. Of these passages, Professor Muir observes: "The word mridavach., which I have translated as 'injuriously speaking,' is explained by the Sayana as meaning one whose organs of speech are destroyed."

The original meaning of the ex-impression was, doubtless, that the language of the Asuras was unintelligible to the Aryas. The same explanation will apply to another passage in the Rig Veda, where it is said: "May we (by propitiating Indra) conquer the ill-speaking man." "The Asuras, being deprived of speech, were undone, crying, 'He lava' He lava,' such was the incomprehensible speech that they uttered," according to the Satapatha Brahmana. It is a Mlecha who speaks in this way. Therefore, since the Asuras speak in such a language, no Brahman can speak in such a barbarous manner. Mann tells us that the Dasyus are the tribes that do not belong to the classes created from the mouth, arms, thighs, and feet of Brahman, regardless of whether they speak the Mlechase or Aryana language. Therefore, both the Mlechas', or Asuras,' language and the Aryan language were spoken during Manu's time. But during the period recounted in the Mahabharata, the Asura language must have all but vanished from the Aryan tribes since Vidura "dressed Yudishthra in the Mlecha tongue, so that all could understand but Yudishthra." However, the grammarian Rama Tarkavagisa speaks of "those who speak like Nagas" later. Long after their converted brethren had cast them aside, the unregenerate Asuras continued to follow their ancestors' religion, language, and customs. These non-regenerate tribes, among which the Dravidian Pandyas were, were clearly speaking the Paisachi dialects.

The fact that the language of the Brahuis, a tribe on the borders of Sind, has been found to be very closely allied to theirs strongly supports the view that the Tamil and cognate tongues were founded upon the ancient Asura speech. Indeed, as Dr. Caldwell states, "We can trace the Dravidian race beyond the Indus to the southern borders of Central Asia thanks to the Brahui (language)." As I have already mentioned, this region was home to the Asuras, or Nagas, whose race appears to have been the ancestors of the founders of the Dravidian kingdom. The only conclusion that can be drawn after taking into account all of the evidence that has been presented is that the Dravidians of southern India were descended from the same stock as the Asuras or Nagas of northern India. Legend and indigenous historians attribute the development of Bunnah and other Indo-Chinese nations to invaders from India; these people are related to the Naga people of Magadha and the north and west of India; the ancient navigators, too, who brought the religions of Brahman and Buddhism, the worship of the Naga, and the Sanskrit or Pali language to Java, Sumatra, and even to distant Celebes, were Indians; they were also probably descended from those Asura dwellers in the ocean, who are mentioned in the Mahabharata and previously discussed. Adventurers, both military and mercantile, found their way to Burmah and the countries beyond from Tamralipti, now Tamluk, and from other ports on the Bay of Bengal; the traditions that speak of them and the sculptured remains that they have left behind show that many, if not most, of these were of the Naga race.

Statue of the Snake Goddess in an Indian temple, Gujarat

The Maharajaweng informs us that Abhi Raja left Kapilavastu and settled in Burmah; his son Kan Rajagyi succeeded him; the Tsin dynasty overthrew it; the king fled to Male, where he passed away; and his queen then wed Daza Raja, an Indian who founded the city of Pagan.

The names of the country of Kambodia (Kamboja), the river Irawadi (Iravati), and several ancient cities in Siam and Burma are Indian in origin. The name of the great serpent temple in Cambodia, Nakhonvat, is merely a corruption of Nagavati. Western India appears to have colonized the islands of the Indo-Chinese Archipelago to a great extent, and here, too, the earlier adventurers appear to have been worshippers of the sun and the serpent. The success of the Buddhist missionaries sent to these countries by Asoka was largely due to the good offices of their fellow citizens who had already settled there. The district of Basuki (Vasuki) and the river Sindhu are located on the island of Bali, close to Java, where Hinduism is still practiced. The island was named after the great Daitya Raja of Patala, and some of its temples feature images of the Naga demi-god Vasuki, along with Garuda and other Hindu deities. There are other temples, the priests of which are Brahmans, and at these, the ceremony is more like that of orthodox Brahmanical temples in India. The ritual at the Naga and Deva temples appears to be much the same as that in use in the Himalayas, which has already been described. At these temples, too, we find the inspired prophet, here called Munku, who is not of Brahman caste and who is the mouthpiece of the city.

The hooded serpent, also known as Naga in these nations, was highly revered. In Bali, during the funeral rites of a man belonging to the Kshatriya caste, a representation of a serpent, called Naga, is carried in the procession and burned alongside the corpse. The Saka-kala, which is so well known and is still in use in parts of Western India and the Himalayas, is another indication of the ancient connection of these islands with India. According to a Javan tradition, a son of the king of Kujrat (Gujrat) led an expedition from India that arrived at 011 on the island's west coast around the year 603, after which other Hindus followed, and a great trade was established with the ports of India and other countries. 1 However, there is no reason to suppose that this was the first arrival of Indian voyagers in the archipelago. A Gujarati proverb states: "He who goes to Java never comes back; but if he does return, his descendants, for seven generations, live at ease." Expeditions to Java are still associated with traditions in Western India. In Marwar, the bards have a legend about Bhoj. Enraged, Raja, the great Puar chief of Ujaini, drove his son Chandrabhan away, and the latter sailed to Java. According to Mr. Kennedy's evidence, as early as the seventh century B.C., Dravidian traders conducted a substantial seaborne trade from Indian ports.

Garuda fights a pair of snakes, Hoysalesvara Temple, Halebid, Karnataka, 12th Century, Shiva temple.

On the other hand, Dravidian navigation dates much earlier than this. As we've seen, the western Indian tribes of the Solar or Naga were prominent in the seaborne trade from very early on. We already know that the legend of "the churning of the ocean" is an allegorical depiction of this, but until much later on, we have no comprehensive accounts of ocean voyages. However, Sakya Buddha himself speaks of such journeys. He states: Historically, seafaring traders had a custom of plunging into the ocean and bringing a shore-spotting bird with them. They would release the shore-sighting bird once the ship was out of sight of land. It would travel to the north, west, and south, as well as to the points in between, before rising high. Should it glimpse land on the horizon, it would proceed in that direction. However, if not, it would return to the ship.

It will be noted that this method of determining a ship's position at sea, which is like the sending out of the birds from the Ark, is said to have been the custom "long ago." Other and more scientific methods were in use in the fifth century B.C., and ocean navigation was already an established institution at that time. In the time of the Chinese Buddhist pilgrim Fah Rian (about 406 A.D.), there was a regular and evidently old-established trade between India and China and with the islands of the Archipelago. Fah Hian sailed from Tamalitti, or Tamralipti, at the mouth of the Ganges in a great merchant ship and, in fourteen days, reached Ceylon. From there, he sailed in a great ship, which carried about two hundred men and was navigated by observing the sun, moon, and stars. On this ship, Fah Rian reached Yc-po-ti (probably Java), in which country heretics and Brahmans flourished, but the law of Buddha was not much known. Here, the pilgrim embarked for China on board another ship carrying two hundred men, among whom were Brahmans. These proposed to treat the sramana as Jonah was treated, and for the same reason, but some of those on board took his part. At length, when their provisions were nearly exhausted, they reached China. All these ships appear to have been Indian and not Chinese. Fah Hian mentions that pirates were numerous in those seas,' which shows that commerce must have been considerable.

The Indian Shiva Temple

6. DEVAS AND NAGAS

According to Brahminic authorities, both Buddhism and Jainism had their roots in the worship of the sun and the serpent. According to legend, after the Daityas defeated them under the leadership of Harada, son of Hiranyakasipu, the Devas begged Vishnu. The god heard their prayers and promised to help, so he sent a great delusion in the form of a naked mendicant, with his head shaved and his body covered in hair. Carrying a bunch of peacock feathers to trick the Daityas. As a result of their seduction from the Vedic religion, they were dubbed Arhatas. Now, it appears that this passage alludes to the Jainas, who were known as Arhatas and were nude ascetics. Furthermore, it is stated that the Daityas were corrupted to the point where none of them acknowledged the Vedic authority and that the same deceiver, dressed in clothing of "red color, assumed a benevolent aspect," spoke to the other members of the family in amiable and gentle tones, leading them to stray from their religious obligations and become Buddhas (Buddhists). The original Digambara Jainas are clearly mentioned in the just quoted passages; the later Swetambara, or white-robed sect, needs to be mentioned. This suggests that the legend is very old. We are told on Brahmanical authority, of rajas who, in ancient times, resigned sovereignty to their sons and retired to the forest to lead a life of asceticism. Thus, Agnidhra, grandson of Manu, his son Nabhi, Rishaba, son of Nabhi, and his son Bharata, are all said to have given up their thrones and become hermits; of these, Rishaba is called an Arbat' and is said to have died naked. The Jainas claim him and Sumati, his grandson, as Tirthakaras, or deified anchorets of that sect.

Brahmanical sources also tell us that some royal house devotees, like Sakya Buddha, renounced their right to succeed to their fathers' thrones in order to live ascetic lives. Notable examples include Yati, son of Yayati and brother of Nahush, who refused to reign and became a son of Pratipa, who gave up the throne to his younger brother Santanu and became a hermit. Jaina devotees are still referred to as Yatis. The Siddhas, who are identified as divine entities with the Devas and the Nagas, were elevated to the status of unis, or ascetics. These include Hara, Visvamitra, Vyasa, Vashista, and Kapila. Khwaja is specifically mentioned as having the right to obligatory worship. Therefore, at that time, both Brahmans and Kshatriyas must have been included in the Siddhas. "Among the Siddhas, I am Kapila Muni," Krishna declares in the Bhagavad Gita. However, Kapila Muni seems to have been the same as Kapila, king of the Nagas.

Before the great war of the Nagas, their tirtha at Kapilavastn was a hallowed site of pilgrimage. Mahabharata, and clearly prior to Krishna's time. Had Kapil Muni not been one of the most renowned ascetics among the Siddhas, it is highly unlikely that Krishna would have drawn comparisons between himself and him. But this Muni was both an Asura and a Naga, having once ruled the Nagas of Patala. Among the Danavas, there is a mention of a Kapila, possibly the same one. The statement "Kapila, the most righteous of saints, he whom the great saints name as Kapila Vasudeva, ruled over the Nagas in Patala and destroyed the 60,000 sons of Sagara when they invaded his dominions, is now worshipped," however, does not clarify whether or not this was Kapila Muni. It is a pair of human feet carved on a rock or on a stone tablet. Between the feet, there might be a representation of the short crutch that followers of the religion use to support themselves while meditating. This foot emblem, known as the Siddh-pat, is a popular place of worship in the Kangra Valley and other areas bordering the Himalayas.

The Siddhas are offered fruit, flowers, and grains; however, neither dancing nor music are typically associated with their worship, nor are animals offered as sacrifices. Like other divinities, they are worshipped with votive offerings, which usually consist of small wooden replicas of sandals or human feet. In certain places, a simple round stone called a pinda, placed under a tree, represents the Siddhas; it is colored white, as opposed to the red that is used for most other deities' symbols. The Siddhas were frequently worshipped as household gods, and the pilgrim's mark, or "Likhnu," is a crude representation of a pair of human feet. The pilgrimage to the Siddha shrines is a very old practice. It is actually a way to honor the deceased. As a result, the Buddha's disciples accepted it as a tribute to their esteemed teacher. In the Himalayas, the impersonation of a pair of human feet carved upon a bridge over a stream or a resting place for travelers erected in honor of some wealthy villager is thought to represent the footprints of the departed, just as the human head carved upon a post personifies the living donor of a similar gift for the public benefit.

Carving details on the outer wall of Hazara Rama Temple.

In the village of Dosun in the upper Sutlej valley, a stone tablet carved with a pair of human feet serves as the shrine for Gobind, the revered Sikh Guru. The footprint arc is still used as a memorial to religious devotees.

As we just saw, Brahmanical writers claimed that the Jainas, who were Asuras, called their deified ascetics Siddha. Of the twenty-four Tirthakaras, or deified anchorites of the Jainas, all were Kshatriyas, and twenty-two of them were of the solar race of Ikshvaku. No wonder, then, that they were closely connected with the sun and the serpent. The last of the Tirthakaras, Vardhamana, or Mahabir, was a contemporary of Sakya Buddha. He was Bimbisaro, the raja of Maghada's spouse's brother, and the son of Siddartha, the raja of Konigamma, close to Vaisali. By permission of his elder brother, Vardhamana became an ascetic; after one year, he went naked; after twelve years, he became a Jina or Tirthakara and was called Mahabir. After his death, he became a Siddha. ' Parswa, the Tirthakara who preceded Mahabir, was a son of Aswasena, raja of Benares. He is always represented with the seven hoods of a Naga expanded over his head. Fergusson found the serpent in all the Jaina temples at Abu. And the colossal Jama statues.

Nagas are present in southern India at Yannur and Sravana Belgola. It has often been noted that serpent worship was closely associated with Buddha and Buddhism; in fact, anyone interested in the topic could easily persuade themselves of this by looking at Fergusson's exquisite photos of the Amravati sculptures or by looking at the sculptures themselves at the British Museum. Sakya Buddha descended from Ikshvaku, was of the solar race, and was given shelter and protection by the Naga raja Muchalinda at the beginning of his religious career. He maintained friendly relations with the Naga people throughout his life, and after his death, the Naga Rajas claimed to have shared his relics and had constructed stupas over them. How close was the relationship between Buddhism and these Asuran descendants? We can see from the sculptures of Amravati, Sanchi, and other places that the Naga people are depicted as worshipping Buddha or Buddhist emblems, and in some cases, these emblems are shown as being worshipped in the same temple as the Naga. In several of the Amravati sculptures, the serpent takes pride in the dagoba, a position that is usually assigned to Buddha himself. Some of these sculptures depict Buddha with his head covered by the extended hoods of a seven-headed Naga, which was, as we've seen, the defining characteristic of a Naga raja.

The Amravati bas-reliefs also depict the Sun, the Trisul, and other solar emblems as objects of Buddhist worship. Buddhist sramanas can be found performing rituals and worshiping the Naga at Nuga temples, even during the Chinese pilgrimage period. In addition to what has already been mentioned, we discover that the followers of Buddha referred to him as Mahanago or the great Naga. It is not difficult to explain all this, for we learn from Brahmanical and Buddhist authorities that the tribe to which Buddha belonged was of the solar race. The Sakyas were descendants of Vaku, the raja of Patala. Sakya, his father Suddhodana, and his son Rahula are said in the Puranas to be of the race of Ikshvakn, too. According to Buddhist records, one of the kings of Patala of this race, having promised the succession to the throne to a younger son by a favorite wife, sent away his elder sons to provide for themselves. These, during their travels, came to Kapilavastu. Here was the tirtha, or shrine, of the great ascetic Kapila Muni, who had been, as we have already seen, king of the Nagas of Patala and was doubtless an ancestral deity. The sons of the King of Patiala settled at Kapilavastu, and their descendants remained in possession until the time of Buddha. Virudhaka Raja then destroyed the city, killing all of the Sakyas except for Buddha and four others. One of those who escaped became raja of Udyana and married a Naga princess, over whose head appeared the nine hoods of a serpent.' This Sakya chief of Udyana, Uttara Sena, who has already been referred to, received a share of the relics of Buddha, over which he built a stupa.

The proof that both Buddha and the Sakyas belonged to the Naga or solar race, has been remarkably reinforced in recent times. When the stupas built over the Sakya relics—killed when the king of Magadha destroyed Kapilavastu—were opened in 1898, the image of a Naga was discovered in almost every relic casket. Among these was a golden Naga named Mahanaman, who was a member of Buddha's own family and the heir Gautama would have shared if he hadn't given up the world. As demonstrated in the pages before, the hooded serpent, also known as the Naga or cobra, was revered in India as the protector, or totem, of a people who claimed ancestry from the Sun god, and it was always connected to Sun worship. Additionally, it has been demonstrated that the leaders of the solar race were revered as gods or demigods after their deaths. These demi-gods were typically depicted with the hoods of shielding serpents spread over their heads. Furthermore, we have seen that many of the solar kings, especially those who claimed paramount power, received divine honors while living as incarnations of the sun god and that, in this capacity, they were believed to have control over the elements and other supernatural powers. It has also been painted out that these deified chiefs were the Nagas of Swarga (Indra's Heaven) and of the epic poems, the celestial serpents being Surya (the Sun) of the Brahmanical writers and the Naga rajas of Indian folklore.

Lepakshi Temple in Andhra Pradesh

It has been demonstrated that in order to win the serpent deities' favor, They were offered sacrifices, and a large number of these victims were people. Despite appearing to have originated in Asia, serpent worship was not limited to India. As in India, so too in other countries; the Serpent was worshipped as the protector, or totem, of people who claimed solar descent; furthermore, the worship of the Sun and the Serpent was conducted everywhere with the same, or nearly the same, rites and ceremonies as those now, or formerly, existing in India. The hooded serpent was held sacred wherever the Sun was worshipped, and the people or their rulers claimed descent from the Sun god. The combined worship of the Sun and the serpent gods must have spread from a common center through migration or communication with the people who claimed solar descent. To the highest degree, it is improbable that this close connection between the Sun and the Serpent could have originated independently in countries as far apart as China and the West of Africa or India and Peru. And it seems scarcely possible that, in addition to this, the same forms of worship of these deities and the same ritual could have arisen spontaneously among each of these far-off peoples.

The Naga was the first totem of the people who claimed ancestry from the Sun god because it was so widely revered. Like the hooded serpent, the tortoise was a very ancient totem of the solar race and is revered in many nations for always being connected to the sun. It is discovered that the worship of the Sun and the Serpent was already in existence, and in fact fully developed, at the earliest dawn of history; no attempt will be made here to trace its spread throughout the ancient world, but it is still practiced, or at least has left its mark, in many countries outside India; a few of these will be mentioned in passing. As has already been mentioned, there was sun and serpent worship in these far-off countries between the Euphrates and the Indus. Persian authors have described the battles fought in this region between the Iranians and the Azi Dahaka dynasty and the Aryans and the serpent race of Ahi as they occurred in the Veda. The Yezidis, or so-called "devil worshippers" of the Zagros mountains, are likely a remnant of the ancient Medic or Proto-medic inhabitants; they still worship the sun god, pray toward the rising sun, and have the serpent carved upon their sacred buildings. Traces of the worship of the sun and the serpent still remain in these ancient seats.

It is likely that in the very early days of Babylonia, as well as in the neighboring countries, the predominant religion was the worship of the sun and the serpent, even though there were many modifications made later on. Ea, the god of the Euphrates River, one of the great serpents' rivers, was among the first gods of Babylonia. His emblem was the seven-headed serpent. The Chaldeans invoked Hea, or Ea, and his son Marduk as the gods of wisdom to protect them from all infernal powers, from sorcery, and from dangers of every kind. According to the Chaldean account of the Deluge, Ea directed the preparation of the ark or ship and gave warning of the impending flood; it is also said that Ea declared this to his minister, who heard it. And he declared the instructions to the Chaldean Noah, Atrahasis, the man of Surippak. Numerous people worship the deity Ea, and Dusratta, King of Mittani, specifically refers to Ea as "Lord of all" in a letter he wrote to King Amenophis III of Egypt. The hooded serpent is not a Semitic totem. The Babylonians appropriated it with the aid of the ancient Accad or Sumerian religion; the Hebrews, for whom the serpent represented evil except in one famous case, did not embrace it. In Babylonia, the serpent remained associated with the sun even in later times, as Nebuchadrezzar tells us, having placed images of poisonous snakes at the gates of the great temple of Marduk, the sun god of Babylon.

All of the Turanian tribes that lived in the area south and west of the Caspian refer to the sun by a variety of names, and the serpent gods are most likely their main deities. We are told that Vishnu was worshipped as the sun in Sakadwipa. ' It may be noted that Suriash, the name of the Kassite Sun god, closely resembles that of Surya, one of the names of the Sun god of the Hindus. A deity named Suriha is also mentioned in Assyrian inscriptions and appears to be the same as Aa or Ea, who, as we have just seen, was the father of Marduk, the Sun-god of Babylon, and possibly was the Sun-god himself. He was probably also the same as the Indian Vishnu. The ancient Chaldean epic poem, whose hero is Izdubar, or Gilgamesh, sheds much light on the religion of Elam. Humbaba, King of Elam, invaded Chaldea and destroyed the country of the Euphrates, according to the poem. Gilgamesh, King of Uruk or Erech, and Eabani, likely the leader of a nearby pastoral tribe, launched an invasion into Elam, where they ambushed and killed Humbaba at the sanctuary of Lrnini, on "the hill of cedars, the abode of the gods." The heroes were greatly impressed by the splendor of the sacred cedars within Humbaba's dominions. After Gilgamesh disobeyed the goddess Ishtar on his triumphant return to Uruk, she cursed him and gave him a skin condition. 1 In order to recover from this illness, the hero traveled to the home (or shrine) of his god and Atrahasis, also known as Shamash-napishtim or Utu-napishtim, the King of Shuruppak who was saved during the Deluge in the ark and who has already been mentioned.

The pilgrimage involved both land and river or sea travel. Gilgamesh recovered after following his ancestor's advice and taking a bath in holy water, and Shamash-Utnapishtim, or possibly the temple priest, then gave him a branch of the tree of life. While drinking at a spring on his way home, Gilgamesh landed on the shore of what appears to have been a hostile nation;

the genius (or deity) of the spring then grabbed a branch of the tree of life. After muttering a curse, the serpent carried the branch away, and Gilgamesh, distraught at his loss and unable to find it, started back home. This description makes it clear that springs were revered by the serpent gods in very early times in the southern countries that bordered the Persian Gulf, just like they are in India. Though the events mentioned in the Chaldean epic took place much earlier, the epic is thought to have been written around 2000 B.C. Worshippers of the Sun and the Serpent in the Himalayas still engage in a number of the religious practices described in the Chaldean poem, including pilgrimages to the shrines of deified ancestors, sheltering temples in cedar groves, and decorating them with the horns of animals killed in the chase.

At first, Gilgamesh is a regular mortal, but later on, he seems to have transformed into a god, and his mother is referred to as a goddess. In fact, it appears that he has taken on the persona of the sun god. Perhaps, like a great deal of other solar chiefs, Gilgamesh took on divine honors upon becoming a sovereign in his own right. There's a tablet that was discovered that had prayers addressed to him as a god. As a personification of the Sun god, Humbaba was also the King of Elam, and it seems that Gilgamesh killed him. It should be noted that Gilgamesh's depiction in Chaldean sculpture, with his long, curling hair and broad, bearded face, strongly resembled that of a modern-day Brahili or Baluch chief. The Deluge tradition seems to be another link between the countries south of the Kaspian and the Indian branch of the Solar Race. The Mahabharata, the Puranas, and the Satapatha Brahmana all mention this, albeit with slight modifications. The Asuras brought the legend with them, most likely from their original home.

Remarkably, Mann, a Kshatriya chief, son of the Sun, and ancestor of Ikshvaku and the Indian branch of the Solar race, received the warning of the impending flood instead of the Rishis or the Brahmans. The fish's function in warning Manu, Vaivaswat, or Satyavrata about the approaching flood and in guiding the building of the ship or ark is shared by all the Indian narratives, and it is similar to the role assigned to the god Ea in the Chaldean account of the same event. Furthermore, this deity is shown as having seven heads on occasion but also occasionally taking the shape of a fish. There is no mention of a location in the oldest known version of the Indian legend, the Satapatha Brahmana. There is a story that Manu picked up a fish while doing his morning ablutions. The fish said, "Rear me. I will save them. A flood will carry away all these creatures. Manu placed the fish in a jar; when it grew larger, he removed it to a pond; when it grew still larger, he placed it in the sea. The fish then told Manu to prepare a ship and, when the flood rose, to go into it. Manu did as he was directed, and when the Deluge came, he embarked on the ship.

Ancient Khmer bas relief carving, Devas, angels, pulling on the snake Vasuki.

Legend of the Churning of the Ocean of Milk, Angkor, Cambodia

The fish came to him, and, to a horn upon its head, Manu tied a rope, by which the ship was towed through the flood to the northern mountain. The fish then said, "I have saved you," and directed Manu to fasten the ship to a tree. The legend takes on a more regional tone in the Mahabharata. A fish approached the riverbank and asked to be protected from the other fish, while Manu Vaivaswat is supposed to have been practicing religious asceticism in the Visa forest. As we've already seen, Visala was Naga chief Takshaka Vaisalya's city. When the fish grew into a pond, Manu removed it from the water and put it in a jar. Eventually, to the river and the sea. The fish then warned Manu to construct a sturdy ark, or ship, equipped with a long rope, foretelling the extinction of all living things on Earth due to a flood. "You cannot save yourself from this terrifying flood without my assistance." The fish said to the rishis, "I am Brahma, the lord of all creatures; there is none greater than myself; assuming the form of a fish, I have saved you from this destruction." Manu set out with the seven rishis and all the different kinds of seeds. The fish then took the ark to the Himavat, where it was tied to a tree."

The Bhagavata Purana's legend is specific to southern India. There, Manu, also known as Satyavrata, is referred to as "the lord of Dravkla," and the fish appears in his hands while he is making a water sacrifice in the Kritamala River, which is supposed to originate in the Malabar or Malayan hills. Thus, the event is only mentioned as having happened in India in later versions of the legend, and even then, it refers to different locations. The same flood is undoubtedly mentioned in both the Indian legend and the Chaldean epic, and, likely, this is also the case in Chinese tradition. The fish that saved Manu is said to have been a manifestation of Vishnu in some Hindu accounts of the Deluge. It should be noted in relation to this that the sea, fish, and many-headed serpent were all connected to the Babylonian Hea and the Indian Vishnu. Could it be that they were the same god, going by different names? In many parts of India, fish are considered sacred and are particularly associated with Vishnu. The sun and the serpent were both revered by the Phoenicians. They probably carried the cult from Babylonia to other countries, as the story of Cadmus illustrates. The Phoenicians also revered a large number of other gods, some of whom were undoubtedly of Babylonian descent.

Even after Christianity was introduced, there were still remnants of sun and serpent worship in Syria and other Western Asian countries. In fact, there exists an interesting blend of this ancient religion with the rituals of early Christian, or rather semi-Christian, sects like the Gnostics. Some Gnostics truly worshipped the serpent, some centuries after the Christian era. The ancient worship of the sun and serpent was also a major source of inspiration for the Manichceans. They turned to face the sun in prayer. They said that Christ lived in the sun, left it to dwell on earth, and then went back to the sun. They considered the serpent to be a helpful ally as well. Though it took on its current form during the Christian era, the legend of St. George and the Dragon was most likely based on an earlier tale. From the beginning of recorded history, the Greeks were worshippers of the sun and the serpent. It is said that Cecrops, the first king of Athens, was half-serpent and half-man when he arrived from Egypt. He was deified, as were his successors. It is also said that Cadmus, the Phoenician who founded Thebes, and his spouse Harmonia turned into serpents.

Upon his arrival in Greece, Cadmus discovered that the serpent tribes had already taken over the country, or at least a portion of it. According to a number of authors, the Phoenician chief decided to locate a city upon arriving in Boeotia, following an oracle. While searching for water, they came across a spring, and a massive snake was watching it and devouring anyone who came too close. On the other hand, Cadmus destroys the serpent and establishes Thebes. The worship of many other gods was combined with the Sun and Serpent in ancient Greece, as was the case in Semitic Babylonia, where some of these Greek deities are thought to have originated. In Greece, the serpent was not as closely associated with the sun as it was in Egypt, India, and other places where it was the emblem of the ruling race of the sun. Nonetheless, the serpent was revered as a protector even in ancient Greece. A large serpent served as the Athenian Acropolis' guardian deity. There are remnants of sun and serpent worship throughout almost all of Europe. Its spread was partly attributed to the Phoenicians and the Egyptians, but the migration of other people, who appeared to be of Asian descent, appears to have played a major role in its westward migration.

From the earliest known times, the sun was worshipped in Egypt, and the uraeus, or hooded serpent, was revered, though variations were made during various dynasties. The Sun was said to be the ancestor of the Pharaohs. As an incarnation of the sun god, each reigning king was accorded divine honors during their lifetime. Every individual possessed a temple where their statue was enthroned, gathered devotion, gave prophecies, and performed all the duties of a deity. As was previously mentioned, the Pharaohs wore official regalia that read, "The King, My Lord, My Sun God." The Egyptian province governors also used this form of address when reporting to the King. Every pharaoh was revered as a god after their death. On the front of the king's headdress was a picture of the hooded serpent. This was more than just a royal insignia; it served as a shield and was meant to destroy any assailants to the pharaoh. The sun and the serpent were as closely related in Egypt as they were in other nations whose rulers professed to be descended from the sun.

Bas relief of Lord Vishnu, Five headed snake, Mahabalipuram, Tamil Nadu.

The sun is depicted as standing in his divine bark with the coils of the serpent (Uraeus) surrounding him in a Theban papyrus dedicated to Harmakhis. The sun-worshipping people of Asia were closely related to the Egyptians through social customs and religious rites. Indeed, there is little reason to doubt the Pharaohs' and their followers' Asian ancestry.

Likely, the many animals that the ancient Egyptians worshipped were once totems. Prior to their conversion to Christianity, the Ethiopians, also known as the Abyssinians, were worshippers of the sun and the serpent. When the Ethiopian King was in Heliopolis, he served as a priest at the sun temple. The Ethiopian kings were accorded divine honors, just like the Pharaohs and other leaders of the Solar Race. The Ethiopians were known to the Egyptians as Kaushu or Kush, a name that alludes to the Kashshu, or Kassites, of the region east of the Tigris. Indeed, Lepsius and others have held that Kaushu originated in Asia and was related to the races of Elam. Regarding this, it should be mentioned that the title of Negi, held by the chiefs of the Khus tribes of the Himalayas, seems to be closely associated with that of Negis, the King of Abyssinia.

The nation of Pilanit, or Punt, which bordered Ethiopia and appears to have included the islands and shores of the Red Sea, was said to be home to serpents by the Egyptians. According to a historical papyrus that Golenischeff translated, the great serpent-like chief of Puanit informed an Egyptian shipwrecked mariner that a ship would be arriving from his country in four months. And that he would arrive home after a two-month journey. Consequently, there had to have been frequent trade between Egypt and this land of snakes. The worship of the sun and serpents continued in a very primitive form into our own times and is hardly extinct in the kingdoms of Western and Central Africa, except for those regions where Mohammedanism had replaced it. The true purpose of the Ju-Ju, or Fetish, rituals in these nations was to worship the Sun, the Serpent, and the gods of kings and ancestors.

Except for Mexico, the extent of human sacrifices and other atrocities committed here is unmatched by any other region of the world. Among the solar race's sacred totems were the tortoise and the snake. Every significant transaction was made with an offering to the serpent, a tutelary deity that was present everywhere. Most, if not all, of the cabalistic signs that the priests employed for magical purposes were the same as those found in India and other Asian nations that worship the sun. It remains to be seen how sun and serpent worship came to be practiced in these nations. However, it ruled over a sizable portion of Africa prior to the arrival of Mohammedanism. It is highly unlikely that it originated in the African tribes; instead, it originated in

Asia. However, some of the lesser deities were likely descended from native people. Worshiping the Sun and the Serpent is still very common and is the oldest religion that people can still remember in China and the surrounding countries. Similar to India and other nations, it is connected to the veneration of heavenly ancestors. It is said that the Chinese Emperor is the son of heaven or, more accurately, the highest god. While still alive, he is accorded divine honors, and upon his death, he is revered as a god."

As he has since the beginning of Chinese history or legend, the Naga, or dragon, continues to guard the empire, ruling over the elements and receiving official worship during periods of floods or drought. There are many shrines dedicated to Naga Raja, the Dragon King, or Lung Wang. In addition, tortoises are revered, and their shells are used as oracles. The Chinese army commander's emblem was a banner with a tortoise and a serpent on it. Chinese historians have described half-serpent, half-man mythological emperors among their early rulers. Taihao, Paohsi, or Fushi possessed the virtues of a sage, the body of a serpent, and the head of a man. Another divine king, Shennung, also known as "the blazing god," was born under the influence of a sacred dragon. He had the body of a man and the head· of an ox, or rather perhaps of a bull. His successor, Ntikua, had the body of a serpent, the head of a man, and the virtue of a holy man. According to M. Terrien de Lacouperie, China's civilization originated in the West and was a branch of an extremely old civilization that was supposedly rooted in the region between the Caspian Sea and the Persian Gulf. Other distinguished scholars have yet to unanimously agree with all of these viewpoints.

As we've seen, the Dravidian civilization of India and the associated sun and serpent worship originated in the just-mentioned region. The lake, which sits in the crater of the holy "Ever White Mountain," is sacred to Lung Wang, the dragon king; the people of Manchuria belong to the solar race, and the Naga demi-gods still rule the rivers and the rain. In Korea, people eat, worship, and revere serpents as the guardian genii of their homes; the kings are descended from the sun and are shielded by the dragon. The sun god is now a goddess in Japan. The Mikado is a divine being who is descended from the Sun goddess in an uninterrupted line. Japanese chronicles describe the mountain gods as serpentine creatures. The ritual associated with the worship of the sun and serpent in these nations was identical to that practiced in India in all material respects. During the early centuries of the Christian era, Chinese Buddhist pilgrims traveling to India discovered that the Naga demi-gods controlled all the rivers and lakes in the nations they traveled through. The Lu or Naga demi-gods are still in charge of Thibet's springs, rivers, and lakes. In the depths of Lake Palti, there is a crystal palace home to a Naga king.

Naga Stone Statue on Kampong Kdei Bridge, Cambodia

The sick Grand Lama of Tashilunpo was supposed to have been offended in some way when he bathed in Barchutsan's hot springs in 1882, and the lamas organized religious ceremonies honoring the serpent deities as a result. Buddhist priests continue to oversee the worship of the serpent gods in Thibet, as we have seen in India. Sun and serpent worship was widespread on the American continent during the Spanish invasion, and it seems to have taken exactly the same form as it did in the old world, with the exception that the native rattlesnake took the place of the hooded serpent, which did not exist in America, and still possessed all the characteristics associated with the Naga in the old world. Atahualpa, the Inca, most likely chose this meeting spot in the hopes of receiving protection from his ancestral deity, the Serpent, a stone serpent. Pizarro met the Inca at Cassamarca, Peru.

The tortoise, considered one of the earliest totems of the solar race and strongly associated with the sun and serpent worship of the other hemisphere, was also considered sacred by American sun worshippers. Both the tortoise and the serpent had human heads, indicating that they were revered as totems rather than just reptiles; in fact, they served as both the race's protectors and ancestors both here and in the ancient world. The sun and serpent are worshipped with the same rites and ceremonies in both Asia and America. Additionally, both regions had people who were members of the solar race who worshipped the serpent: kings who claimed divine honors while alive as the sun god personified and who were worshipped as deities after death. The laws, social mores, and other customs that were in place in America at the time of its discovery were also strikingly similar to those of the sun-worshipping nations of the old world, indicating—as several writers have suggested—that the religion and civilization of the Indian nations of America have their origins in Asia. It looks like even the scalping knife and laso are from Asia.

As we've seen, those who claimed to be descended from the Sun god revered the hooded serpent as a sacred totem, eventually leading to its worship as a deity. Furthermore, it appears that the worship of heavenly bodies, kings, totems, and ancestors—all of which gave rise to numerous gods associated with the Sun—as well as the ritualistic offering of human sacrifice and other atrocious acts in certain Sun-worshipping nations, originated as corrupt forms of devotion to a supreme deity believed to reside in the Sun. It is forbidden to utter the Gayatri, the most revered passage in the Veda, in a way that could be overheard. The core of Hinduism is a brief prayer to the Sun god, also known as Savitri, the generator or Creator. Other ancient cultures, including the early Egyptians, revered the sun god as the Creator.

Naga in front of Prasat Hin Phanom Rung, Thailand

Naga engraved by a magnificent sandstone to create a railing.

Snake stone statue, Beng Mealea Khmer temple, Cambodia

The Naga Bridge, Phimai Historical Park, Thailand

Naga or large Snake Engraved, front, and back profile.

Bangalore, Karnataka, India, Sheshnaga, Muthyala Eshwara temple, Pearl Valley

King of Nagas in Chiang Rai province, Thailand

Phanom Rung Historical Park Naga staircase five-headed.

Bas relief Naga, Mahabalipuram, Tamil Nadu.

Phanom Rung in Buriram, Thailand

Hindu goddess, Buddha Park, Vientiane, Laos

Dancers and Nagas Sun Temple in Konark, India.

India Shravanabelagola, altar with a statue of God Vishnu.

APPENDICES

APPENDIX 1: NAGAS

The term "Naga" originates from Sanskrit and means serpent. In religions like Jainism, Buddhism, and Hinduism, it denotes a mythical entity that is part snake and part human. Nagas are known for their beauty and strength, possessing the ability to morph into entirely human or snake forms. While they can be perilous, they often assist humans. They dwell in an underground realm called Naga-loka or Patala-loka, filled with lavish palaces decorated with precious gems. The creator god Brahma, due to the growing population of Nagas on Earth, exiled them to the north, instructing them to bite only the truly wicked or those fated to die prematurely. They are known as protectors of treasure and are associated with various water bodies like lakes, rivers, seas, and wells.

Key figures among the Nagas include Vasuki, used as a rope in the churning of the cosmic ocean; Takshaka, the snake tribe's leader; and Shesha (or Ananta), who supports Narayana (Vishnu) in the Hindu creation story. Naga-Panchami, a festival in modern Hinduism celebrating serpent birth, occurs in the Shravana month (July-August). Nagini or Nagi, the female counterparts, are mesmerizing serpent princesses. Their unions with humans are said to have founded the dynasties of Manipur, the Pallavas, and the royal family of ancient Funan (Indochina). In Buddhism, Nagas often guard doors or, in Tibetan tradition, serve as minor deities. A notable example is the depiction of Naga king Muchalinda sheltering Buddha during meditation, seen in Mon-Khmer Buddhas from the 9th-13th century in Thailand and Cambodia. Jainism portrays the Tirthankara Parshvanatha with a canopy of

Naga hoods over his head. Artistically, Nagas are represented in three forms: fully serpent-like, human with a hood canopy, or half-human with a coiled lower body. They are often shown in adoration, witnessing miracles performed by major gods or heroes.

Nagas, as serpent spirits from the underworld, can be traced back to around 2500 BCE during the Indus Valley civilization. According to Hindu Puranic legends, they descend from Kadru, sister of Vinata and mother to the multi-headed serpents in Patala and adversaries of Garuda. This underground kingdom, rich in treasures, is ruled by notable Naga kings like Sesha, Vasuki, and Takshaka. The Nagas have left an indelible mark on Indian culture through serpent worship. In Buddhism, Nagas inherit significant symbolism from ancient Indian traditions. They reside beneath the Earth and oceans, especially in water realms. Buddhist cosmology places them at the lowest tier of Mt. Meru, below their Garuda enemies. Nagas can morph into serpentine, half-serpentine, or human forms and are custodians of esoteric teachings and treasures. The Buddhist philosopher Nagarjuna is said to have received the Prajna-paramita-sutra from them.

Nagas interact with humans in various ways, including controlling weather and causing diseases due to environmental disrespect or pollution. Buddhism recognizes eight great Naga kings, often depicted in stories as ornaments or under the feet of wrathful gods. A five-caste system, paralleling the Hindu hierarchy, categorizes Nagas based on color and direction, with each caste associated with specific colors and positions in the Five Buddha mandala. Nagas are usually depicted iconographical with a human upper body and a serpentine lower half. They are often white, with hands in prayer or holding jewels, and with a serpent hood of one to seven snakes overhead, representing the great Naga kings or the five castes. The multiheaded serpent motif may originate from the ancient River Indus's estuaries. The iconography of Nagas typically presents them with a human torso and a serpentine lower body. Commonly, a Naga is portrayed with a single face and two arms, predominantly in white. Their hands might be clasped in devotion or clutching precious stones. Above their heads, a canopy composed of one, three, five, or seven smaller serpents emerges, often in varied hues to symbolize the eight distinguished Naga kings or the five Naga castes. The imagery of a multi-headed serpent adorning the Indian Naga’s head could possibly have its roots in the depiction of the seven or nine deltas of the ancient River Indus.

APPENDIX 2: HINDUISM

Hinduism is a well-known world religion that originated on the Indian subcontinent and includes a variety of belief systems, rituals, and ways of thinking. Even though British writers first used the term "Hinduism" in the early 19th century, it refers to a long-standing tradition of texts and practices, some of which date back to the second millennium BCE or even earlier. According to academics, Hinduism may be the oldest religion in the world if Hindu traditions originated in the Indus Valley civilization (3rd–2nd millennium BCE). Its many sacred writings in Sanskrit and other regional languages, along with rituals and the visual and performing arts, have played a major role in the religion's globalization. For more than a millennium, Hinduism primarily impacted Southeast Asia, starting in the fourth century CE.

As of the early 21st century, nearly a billion people worldwide practiced Hinduism, making up approximately 80% of India's population. Hinduism's many regional manifestations offer the greatest understanding of the religion despite its widespread practice worldwide. Following the publication of books like "Hinduism" (1877) by eminent Oxford scholar Sir Monier Monier-Williams, the term "Hinduism" came to be used as a description of religious beliefs and customs exclusive to India. It originated from the historical usage of the term "Hindu," which early Greek and Persian visitors to the Indus Valley used. Originally, it was an external label. Indians gradually started using the term to set themselves apart from Turks in the 16th century, changing its meaning from one of ethnic, regional, or cultural identification to one of religion.

Since the late 19th century, Hindus' responses to the term "Hinduism" have been diverse. Some have chosen to refer to it by their own terms, while others have chosen to refer to it as "Vedic religion," which includes not only the old Vedas but also a wide range of sacred texts and an old way of life. The 19th century saw the rise in popularity of another term, "Sanatana dharma" (eternal law), which emphasized the timeless qualities of the tradition that went beyond regional interpretations. But many people—possibly even the majority—have adopted "Hinduism" or terminology akin to it in different Indian languages, particularly "Hindu dharma" (Hindu moral and religious law). Hindus have been writing about Hinduism under the Sanatana Dharma banner since the early 1900s, continuing a long-standing tradition of elucidating doctrine and practice that dates back to the first millennium BCE. Hinduism's origins go even deeper: from epic and Vedic literature from the second millennium BCE, where commentary schools can be found, to artwork that shows Nagas, or serpent-like deities, and yakshas, spirits associated with locations and natural events, which have been worshipped since approximately 400 BCE. Some people link its origins to female terracotta figurines that may have been goddess representations found at the sites of the Indus Valley civilization.

Hindus are more aware of and appreciative of their traditions' complexity, diversity, and multilayered structure than members of other major religious groups. The Hindu prayer for receiving good thoughts from all directions reflects the common belief that truth cannot be limited to a single doctrine, which is the source of this openness. As a result, Hinduism encourages seeking the truth through diverse sources as opposed to following rigid doctrine. Every individual's understanding of truth, including that of a highly regarded guru, is inherently shaped by various factors: time, age, gender, state of consciousness, social and geographic background, and level of spiritual achievement. These diverse perspectives enrich, rather than diminish, the broader view of religious truth. This leads to a prevailing belief among modern Hindus in the paramount virtue of tolerance. Yet, even cosmopolitan Hindus who are part of a global environment acknowledge the unique development of their religion within the Indian subcontinent. This balance between universalist and particularist tendencies has historically energized the Hindu tradition. When Hindus refer to their faith as Sanatana dharma, they underscore its unbroken, seemingly eternal existence and its encompassment of a network of customs, duties, traditions, and values that extend beyond the Western notion of religion as a belief system. In distancing themselves from this Western perspective, English-speaking Hindus often emphasize that Hinduism is more than a religion; it's a way of life.

In the vast expanse of Indian religious history, at least five elements shape the Hindu religious tradition: doctrine, practice, society, narrative, and devotion. These elements are likened to strands in a complex braid, each evolving from historical dialogues, developments, and challenges. Thus, identifying central points of tension is often more insightful for understanding the tradition than seeking uniform agreement on Hindu thought and practice. The first element, doctrine, is rooted in the vast textual tradition anchored by the Veda ("knowledge"), primarily organized by the learned Brahman class. This element reveals several key tensions: the relationship between the divine and the world, the contrast between the world-maintaining concept of dharma and the liberation-oriented moksha (release from an inherently flawed world), and the conflict between individual destiny shaped by karma (the influence of actions on one's present and future lives) and the deep ties to family, society, and related deities. Practice is the second key element in Hinduism. For many Hindus, practice is of foremost importance. Despite India's vast diversity, a common grammar of ritual behavior connects different regions, social strata, and historical periods. Elements of ancient Vedic rituals persist in modern practices, but a more pervasive aspect is the worship of icons or images (pratima, murti, or archa), broadly termed puja ("honoring the deity").

Performed by priests in temples such as Archana, it mirrors acts of hospitality like offering and sharing food, known as Prasada (meaning "grace"). This ritual symbolizes the reciprocity between humans and deities; by consuming prasada, worshippers acknowledge their dependence on the divine. While the practice of puja and Prasada implies universal equality before God, it has, at times, reinforced exclusionary social norms, creating a point of tension. Society, the third organizing element of Hindu life, has also shaped its religious practices. Historically, visitors to India, from ancient Greeks and Chinese to the Persian scholar Al-Biruni in the 11th century, noted the intricate, hierarchical social structure known as the caste system. This system, comprising varnas (ideal classes) and jatis (endogamous birth groups), reflects a plural and hierarchical Indian society, mirroring a similar understanding of truth or reality. The debate persists on whether religious doctrine influences societal structures or vice versa. The Rigveda's famous hymn (10.90) illustrates this concept, narrating the cosmic sacrifice of Purusha, resulting in a four-part cosmos and a corresponding social order of Brahmans, Kshatriyas, Vaishyas, and Shudras.

Like its religious practices and doctrines, there is a noticeable tension in Hinduism's social sphere. This stems from the notion that every individual or group has a distinct perspective that causes them to perceive reality differently. A society must permit everyone to express their opinions and behave in accordance with them in order for it to accurately reflect truth or reality. But this strategy, which puts emphasis on perspective and context, may unintentionally reinforce privileged and discriminatory social structures. When universal norms are ignored, one group can readily justify its superiority over another. Because of this, even though they support tolerance in matters of doctrine, some Hindus have historically maintained caste distinctions in society.

Another element that ties Hindus together as a community of discourse is narrative. For millennia, stories of supernatural entities and their interactions with humans have captivated different parts of India and, increasingly, other parts of the world. Hindu mythological characters like Krishna and Radha, Rama with Sita and Lakshmana, Shiva, and Parvati (or Sati in a different guise), and the Great Goddess Durga as the warrior who vanquishes the buffalo demon Mahisasura are frequently depicted in these stories. These kinds of stories usually show gods like Rama and Krishna actively participating in human affairs. They delve into topics like human experiences, love, and striking a balance between responsibility and play, chaos and order. Hindus frequently believe that they are a member of a larger, imagined family because of these stories. These stories do, however, also draw attention to moral and societal conflicts. For example, the Ramayana, which normally celebrates Rama's righteousness, is occasionally told from Sita's point of view, highlighting her sufferings. Unlike the stories of upper-caste Sanskrit epics like the Mahabharata, lower-caste musicians in North India reinterpret religious epics to reflect their own societal experiences. These variations give the well-known, predominantly male pan-Hindu narratives more complexity and challenge.

Over time, the Hindu experience has been unified by a fifth element called bhakti, which means "sharing" or "devotion." The writings of India's vernacular poet-saints, who represent a range of genders and social classes, bear witness to this tradition, which is centered around the love of God. Their multilingual devotional poems offer a rich tapestry of feelings and images. Bhakti poetry originated in Tamil, South India, and traveled northward without depending on Sanskrit, the upper caste's traditional language, by overcoming linguistic and chronological barriers. Some poems and themes in the lives of these poet-saints are strikingly similar despite language or historical differences. Bhakti challenges other facets of Hindu life and adds to a shared heritage, including a protest tradition, by prioritizing faith over ritualistic rigidity or doctrinal strictness. However, there are different ways to express bhakti; some are more outspoken in their criticism of idolatry, caste divisions, and the fulfillment of religious vows, fasting, and penance.

Nevertheless, this method has drawbacks because it might inadvertently highlight aspects present in the oldest extant manuscripts, which were primarily preserved by men of higher castes, particularly Brahmans. These texts might not accurately reflect the opinions of women, local communities, or people of lower social status who identify as Hindus today or who belong to groups that fall into the wide Hindu spectrum. As a result, these texts ought to be analyzed critically, taking into account the unsaid viewpoints and ignored rebuttals of these frequently marginalized groups. Hinduism has historically been defined by upper-caste adherents by their veneration of the Vedas, the oldest religious scriptures in India, as the only reliable source of unquestionable truth. The Vedas are also regarded as the source of all later Shastra writings, such as the Ayurveda, which emphasize the religious importance of Brahmans. Most Hindus tend to revere the Vedas from a distance, but most are unaware of their actual contents, even though they are quoted in important Hindu rituals and have influenced much of Hindu thought. Hindus once viewed communities that rejected Vedic authority, such as Buddhists and Jains, as heterodox; however, in modern times, these groups are frequently recognized as belonging to a larger family of Indian traditions.

The standing given to Brahmans as a priestly class regarded as spiritually superior by birth is another noteworthy feature of Hindu philosophy. Brahmans have been linked to ritual purity and social status because they are thought of as the guardians of the Vedas and as embodiments of religious authority. This view has been contested, though, either by competing claims to religious authority—especially from rulers—or by the conviction that real Brahmanhood can only be attained by intense study as opposed to birth. Vedic literature demonstrates this challenge, particularly in the Upanishads and Bhakti texts, which frequently juxtapose the profound spiritual experiences of poet-saints like Kabir and Ravidas with the narrow-mindedness of some Brahmans. The majority of Hindus hold to the idea of Brahman, an uncreated, eternal, infinite principle that encompasses all existence and non-existence. This ultimate reality, which manifests or transforms into the universe or appears as all existence. As the universe's creator, sustainer, transformer, and absorber, Brahman is the true self (atman) of all living things and is present in everything. There are differing views among Hindus regarding which personal deity—Vishnu, Shiva, or Shakti—or impersonal force—Brahma—is the best way to comprehend this ultimate reality. The following three groups tend to lean towards these interpretations: Shaivas, Shaktas, and Vaishnavas. For more than 3,000 years, the quest for knowledge of this one, all-pervasive reality has been a fundamental part of India's spiritual path.

Hindus widely embrace the concept of transmigration and rebirth, paired with the complementary doctrine of karma. Samsara, the name for this endless cycle of rebirth, is a collection of lives connected by ongoing attachments. Actions driven by desire and cravings entangle the soul (jiva) in an unending cycle of birth and death. Desire drives social interactions, especially those involving sex or food, and results in an exchange of both good and bad karma. A common perspective is that salvation, or moksha, signifies liberation from this cycle and the impermanence of worldly existence. Salvation is seen as attaining the one permanent and eternal truth: the One, God, or Brahman, in stark contrast to the transient nature of worldly life. Those who do not recognize their true identity as Brahmans are considered misguided. However, human experience itself guides toward the ultimate realization of the oneness between Brahman and Atman. This realization can be achieved through various means: understanding one's inherent unity with all beings, responding to a personal manifestation of the divine with love, or recognizing that the diverse experiences and states of waking consciousness are rooted in a transcendental unity, glimpses of which are experienced in deep, dreamless sleep.

Hinduism acknowledges several paths (margas) towards this liberation. The influential text Bhagavad-Gita, around 100 CE, outlines three such paths:

- Karma-marga: the path of ritual action or duties involving the selfless fulfillment of ritual and social obligations.
- Jnana-marga: the path of knowledge involving meditative focus and ethical, contemplative training (Yoga) to achieve insight into one's unity with Brahman.
- Bhakti-marga: The path of devotion to a personal God.

These paths are suited to different individuals but are interrelated and accessible to all.

Although Hindu life institutionalizes the pursuit of moksha through ascetic practices and the concept of renouncing worldly life, many Hindus do not strictly follow these practices. The Bhagavad-Gita suggests that since action is unavoidable, the three paths should be viewed as means to simultaneously achieve both worldly duties (dharma) and liberation (moksha). By relinquishing desire and detachment from the outcomes of actions, one can engage fully in life while remaining unattached. This aligns with the real-life goals of most Hindus:

- Fulfilling social and ritual duties
- Supporting one's caste, family, and profession.
- Contributing to the stability of the cosmos, nature, and society

Designating Hinduism as Sanatana dharma underscores this aim of maintaining individual and global balance, highlighting the role of traditional religious practices in achieving it. Universal principles, like ahimsa (the principle of non-harm), are shaped by more specific dharmas that apply to each of the four major varnas: brahmans (priests), kshatriyas (warriors and nobles), vaishyas (commoners), and shudras (servants). This is because no one person can fulfill all the social, occupational, and age-defined roles that are necessary for a healthy life. Additionally, the more specific dharmas of the thousands of distinct castes take precedence over these broader categories, intersected by obligations related to gender and life stage (ashrama). Hence, Hindu ethics is highly context-sensitive, expecting and embracing a diversity of individual behaviors.

European and American academics have frequently overstated the so-called "life-denying" elements of Hinduism, such as the stringent practices of yoga. This dichotomy of asceticism and sensuality reflects in Hindu society as a conflict between the yearning for spiritual liberation and the deep-seated desire to continue the family lineage and partake in worldly life. For many centuries, Hindus have debated the merits of an active life engaged in good deeds (pravritti) versus the renunciation of worldly pursuits (nivritti). Philosophical texts like the Upanishads have emphasized renunciation, while dharma texts advocate for the religious virtue of householders who uphold their ritualistic duties and familial responsibilities. About two millennia ago, these dharma texts formulated the concept of the four ashramas ("stages of life") to reconcile these conflicting aspects of Hinduism. This system proposed that a male of the three higher classes should sequentially progress through being a chaste student (brahmachari), a married householder (grihastha), a forest-dwelling retiree focusing on spiritual pursuits (vanaprastha), and optionally, a wandering ascetic (sannyasin). The stage of the forest dweller, a balance between worldly and spiritual life, was often overlooked or omitted in practice.

While the householder stage was frequently praised, with some authorities deeming it superior and viewing other stages as merely preparatory, there have always been individuals who chose the ascetic path immediately after studentship. Theoretical reconciliations allowed for asceticism to those devoid of worldly desires, potentially bypassing traditional prior stages, as a result of disciplined conduct in former lives. The texts outlining these life stages were written by men for men, largely ignoring equivalent stages for women. For instance, the Manu-smriti (100 CE; Laws of Manu) equated marriage to a woman's initiation, effectively excluding women from the student stage. In the householder stage, a woman's role was predominantly seen as serving her husband. However, historical practices challenge the notion that these patriarchal norms were perfectly implemented or wholly accepted by women. While some women chose asceticism, many more engaged in their religious lives by seeking a state of blessedness that was both worldly and reflective of broader cosmic well-being. Women often harnessed their life-giving force (shakti) for their families' benefit, but this force is also recognized as an independent ideal.

APPENDIX 3: HINDU TEXTS

The oldest books in Hinduism are the Vedas, which are sometimes referred to as "knowledge." They are believed to have been "heard" or divinely revealed by rishis or enlightened seers, who committed them to memory in Sanskrit, which is thought to be the ideal language for humans. Even though later Hindu doctrines and practices have largely eclipsed the religious practices of the Vedic era, which were primarily focused on fire sacrifices, Vedic hymns, or mantras, they still have great religious value. These hymns have remained relevant for millennia because they are regularly chanted at traditional weddings, funerals, and temple ceremonies.

The Rigveda (c. 1500 BCE) and the Upanishads (c. 1000–600 BCE) are examples of Vedic literature, which served as the foundational texts for Indian religion prior to the rise of Buddhism and early classical Hinduism. The four Vedas—the oldest being the Rigveda, which is called "Wisdom of the Verses," the others being the Yajurveda, Samaveda, and Atharvaveda, which is called "Wisdom of the Atharvan Priests"—are the most important of these. The focus of later Vedic texts, such as the Upanishads (esoteric teachings), Aranyakas (Books of the Forest), and Brahmanas (ritual discussions), shifts from the early Rigvedic gods and reduces them to minor roles in Vedic rites. The polytheistic belief system develops into a sacrificial pantheism around Prajapati, the universe's embodiment and "Lord of Creatures." In the Upanishads, Prajapati shifts from particular deities to more abstract philosophical ideas, becoming synonymous with Brahman, the ultimate cosmic entity.

Hinduism regards the entire corpus of Vedic literature—the Samhitas, Brahmanas, Aranyakas, and Upanishads—as the Shruti ("heard") or revealed scripture. All other texts are considered Smriti ("remembered") because they are written by humans and contain the actual doctrines and practices of Hinduism. Although the Vedas are considered an infallible source of knowledge and tradition in Hinduism, there is some wiggle room between Shruti and Smriti. Since the Upanishads have been composed up until recently, the Shruti is not completely closed. Furthermore, Smriti texts frequently assert that they are in harmony with the canonical Shruti, thereby striving for a comparable level of respect. The religion represented in the Rigveda is one that acknowledges a variety of deities, especially those connected to the sky and atmosphere. The Indo-European sky god Dyaus was not as important as other gods such as Indra, Varuna, Agni, and Surya. The main ritual in the Rigveda is the soma sacrifice, which entails creating a hallucinogenic drink from an unidentified plant—possibly a mushroom—and then switching it out for another plant. Animal sacrifice is also mentioned in the Rigveda, and it probably became more popular after that. At first, the barriers separating the priestly class were pliable, permitting non-priestly people to become priests. By the end of the Rigvedic period, however, priests had established a separate class, the Brahmans, and were claiming dominance over other social classes, such as the warrior class known as the Rajanyas (later Kshatriyas).

Though it does not go into great detail about birth rituals, the Rigveda does describe marriage and funerary rites in great detail that are comparable to those that are observed in later Hinduism. The image of marriage is one of an unbreakable bond strengthened by complex and solemn rituals that revolve around the family hearth. Cremation was the primary funeral ritual for the wealthy, despite the existence of other funeral customs. A hymn mentions a custom in which the wife of the deceased lies next to him on the funeral pyre, but she is called back to the living before the pyre is lit, suggesting that there may have once been a custom in which the wife and her husband were cremated. The munis, mystics skilled in magical arts and thought to be capable of supernatural feats like levitation, are also introduced in the Rigvedic religion. They were closely linked to Rudra, a mountain and storm deity who was more hated than worshipped. Rudra later changed into the Hindu god Shiva and rose to prominence. Similar to this, Vishnu—who was first described as a solar deity in the Rigveda—became one of the most revered and significant gods in Hinduism.

Similar to myths from ancient Mesopotamia, one of the most famous Vedic tales is that of Indra slaying the great dragon Vritra. This story and others gradually gave way to more esoteric cosmological theories, as shown in the tenth book of the Rigveda. The goal of these early philosophical endeavors was to reduce everything into one essential idea. The archaeological discoveries of Painted Gray Ware in the western Ganges valley are consistent with the chronology of later Vedic developments, which most likely occurred between 1000 and 500 BCE. These discoveries, which point to a developing civilization without writing, provide only a cursory understanding of the religious customs of the era. Thus, in order to comprehend this religious phase, scholars rely on textual sources.

The Yajurveda and Samaveda serve the Vedic liturgy. The Yajurveda consists of short texts that direct ritual actions and invocations for the executive priest (acharya). The Samaveda is an anthology of Rigvedic verses, along with a few new ones, chanted to distinct tunes. Unlike other Vedic texts, the Atharvaveda consists of 20 books that combine prose and hymns. Magical prayers for various purposes, such as prosperity, long life, healing, and curses, are found in Books 1–7. These stand in contrast to the

Rigveda's emphasis on exalting the liturgy and principal deities. Books 8–12 continue the Rigvedic cosmology and introduce the more complex theories found in the Upanishads. The Atharvaveda is an essential resource for comprehending practical religious practices, particularly when supplementing the Rigveda, as the remaining books cover a variety of topics, including the cosmic principle, marriage rites, and funeral formulas. Many of these rituals are described in detail in the "Kausika-sutra," an Atharvavedic manual written for the Kausika priestly family.

A Brahmana is a collection of expositions on religious rituals found in each Samhita of the Vedas. These texts are an important source for learning about Vedic religion even though they are not practical guides like the later Shrauta sutras. They offer detailed explanations of the execution and meaning of Vedic sacrificial rituals. The act of sacrifice is fundamental to the universe, human affairs, and religious goals in these texts. Offering sacrifices creates karma, which allows the sacrificer to have a second birth in heaven after passing away. It is through the homologies, or connections (bandhas), between the ritual elements and corresponding regions of the universe that the effects of rituals on both the visible and invisible realms are understood. The idea of offering Prajapati ("Lord of Creatures") as a sacrifice serves as an illustration of this cosmic aspect of rituals since it is believed that Prajapati's perpetual regeneration is essential to the sacrifice.

The rajasuya, or royal consecration ceremony, is a noteworthy ritual from this era that highlights royal authority and momentarily elevates the king to divine status. The Ashvamedha, or sacrifice of the horse, is another complex custom. Under the protection of the king's army, a consecrated horse is allowed to roam freely for a year as part of this ritual before being brought back for an intricate sacrificial ceremony in the royal capital. This ceremony emphasizes the authority of the monarch and the sacredness of royal duties. The "Books of the Forest," or Aranyakas, expand on these concepts of cosmic sacrifice. With two different kinds of materials, they talk about rituals that are considered inappropriate for village environments (thus the name "forest") and go deeper into the relationship between sacrifice, the cosmos, and humanity. The creative force underlying ceremonial utterances, known as brahman, is a central idea in these texts. Brahman emphasizes the deep and continuous relationship between human religious activities and the greater cosmic framework. It also denotes the creativeness inherent in sacrifices and underlies both ritualistic and cosmic order.

APPENDIX 4: HINDU HISTORY

The Rigveda, which was mostly written in the latter centuries of the second millennium BCE, is the earliest known written account of Hinduism. The religion that is portrayed in this text is not the same as modern Hinduism; rather, it is a representation of an earlier system of sacrifice called Brahmanism or Vedism that originated among Indo-European-speaking peoples in India. Scholars from the British colonial era postulated that these individuals, who belonged to a group of semi-nomadic and nomadic tribes from southern Russia and Central Asia, carried the Sanskrit language, chariots, and horses with them. These researchers also proposed that related groups that migrated to Europe brought Indo-European languages with them. These theories have been refuted, though, and there is still disagreement over the original Indo-European homeland.

Sanskrit and early Iranian languages are similar, indicating that the Vedic people interacted with early Iranians. Thus, the religion of the Rigveda combines elements shared by early Iranians, elements common to many Indo-European groups, and unique aspects found only in the Indian subcontinent. As a result, Hinduism developed through a variety of sources and the influences of distinct reformers throughout history. Very few aspects of Hinduism's Indo-European origins remain in the religion today. Certain customs from Indo-European cultures can be found in Hindu weddings and ancestor cults, like walking around the sacred fire and practicing domestic fire worship. Other Indo-European elements found in the Rigveda include ritual sacrifices and the worship of male sky gods, such as Dyaus, who is comparable to Zeus in classical Greece and Jupiter in Rome. The Indo-European Valhalla bears similarities to the Vedic conception of heaven.

Practices like the initiation ceremony or "second birth" (upanayana), which involves tying a sacred cord and is shared with Zoroastrianism, and the Vedic deity Varuna, who resembles the Zoroastrian Ahura Mazda, are examples of how Indo-Iranian influence can be seen in later Hinduism. In Hinduism, the sacred drink soma is equivalent to Zoroastrianism's haoma. But the Rigveda also contains elements that are uniquely Indian and not present in Indo-Iranian traditions. There are numerous major gods in the Veda that lack obvious Indo-European or Indo-Iranian equivalents. Certain traits may have evolved within the Vedic framework, but the non-Indo-European inhabitants of the Indian subcontinent are probably responsible for other traits. The word "Dravidian," which is frequently used to characterize these people, designates a family of languages rather than an ethnic community. Some academics hypothesize that the ruling class of the

Indus Valley Civilization spoke a Dravidian language, connecting their script to Dravidian languages. However, there is little evidence to support this theory, and there is scant historical documentation of a pan-subcontinental Dravidian presence.

Hinduism's development can be viewed as a continuous interaction between the religions of various social groups and the upper classes, notably the Brahmans. Since the Vedic period, around 1500 BCE, people across all social strata in the Indian subcontinent have generally sought to align their social and religious practices with Brahmanical norms. This trend was largely driven by the desire of lower-class groups to ascend the social hierarchy by adopting the customs and ideologies of the upper castes. In this process, numerous regional deities were often equated with gods and goddesses from the Puranas. This phenomenon, known as "Sanskritization," began in the Vedic era and likely played a crucial role in spreading the Hinduism of the Sanskrit texts throughout Southeast Asia and the Indian subcontinent. The ongoing conversion of tribal groups to Sanskritization is evidenced by the inclination of some Hindus to associate local and rural deities with the deities of the Sanskrit texts. Sanskritization also encompasses efforts by some Hindus to raise their social status by adopting high-caste practices, such as wearing the sacred cord and practicing vegetarianism.

Sanskritization has been instrumental in unifying diverse regional customs across the subcontinent. Conversely, a process of absorbing and integrating various elements into Hinduism has been equally significant in its evolution. Through this process, many aspects of Hindu mythology and several well-known deities, like Ganesha and Hanuman, were incorporated into Hinduism, often being linked to Vedic gods. Similarly, the veneration of non-Vedic local goddesses contributed to the rise of numerous goddesses now seen as consorts of major male Hindu deities, as well as the worship of individual, unmarried goddesses. Thus, Hinduism's history is marked by the interplay of orthodox practices with broader communal customs and the gradual incorporation of regional traditions by the Brahmans. The prehistoric Indus Valley culture, emerging from the metal-using village cultures in the later centuries of the third millennium BCE, is another significant facet of Hinduism's background. Although there's substantial evidence of the Indus people's material culture, the exact meaning of their civilization remains unclear pending the decoding of their script.

However, some aspects of later Hinduism may trace back to this prehistoric era. Commonly found small terra-cotta figurines of women in village cultures are interpreted as depictions of a fertility deity, a worship practice widespread throughout the Mediterranean and western Asia since the Neolithic era (circa 5000 BCE). The association of this goddess with the bull, a motif also present in ancient religions further west, supports this theory. Archaeological findings from the Harappa culture, which thrived in present-day Pakistan, suggest the possibility of a goddess and bull cult. Various figurines, predominantly of bulls and females, have been unearthed. The bull is notably more common on numerous steatite seals, while female figures appear more frequently as figurines. Some seals display a horned figure, possibly with three faces; on one of these figures, animals are encircling the figure. There are also a few figurines of men, one of whom seems to be dancing, which might represent deities. No structures that can be definitively identified as temples have been discovered at Harappan sites. However, the Great Bath at Mohenjo-Daro and associated ghats, akin to riverbank steps found at later Hindu temples, might have had ritualistic significance. The sophisticated drainage system and prevalence of bathrooms in most houses indicate a strong emphasis on hygiene, possibly more than ritual purity.

The Harappan seals depict scenes that are challenging to interpret but may represent religious or mythical themes, such as trees next to figures possibly symbolizing deities residing within them. The frequently depicted horned figure has been ambitiously interpreted as an early form of the Hindu god Shiva. Bulls are often shown in front of altar-like structures, and while some small conical objects might have been game pieces, they have also been interpreted by some as phallic symbols. If these speculative interpretations are confirmed, they suggest that elements of later Hinduism might have existed 4,000 years ago. Certain aspects of religious life found across India, such as sacred animals, sacred trees (especially the pipal, Ficus religiosa), and the use of small figurines in worship, could have origins in pre-Vedic civilizations. However, given their widespread presence outside India, these elements might also have independently developed within Hinduism.

The early Vedic people, although not leaving extensive material artifacts, bequeathed the Rigveda, a crucial literary record. Comprising ten books, with the first and the last being the most recent, the Rigveda contains 1,028 hymns. A typical hymn includes an exhortation, a main section with prayers, praise, and petitions often linked to the deity's mythology, and a specific request. The composition of the Rigveda likely spanned several centuries and is not a singular work. Its final edition, usually dated to around 1200 BCE, represents a complex religious system. This system was further elaborated over the next few centuries with the addition of three more Vedas and subsequent Vedic literature like the Upanishads and the Brahmanas.

Between 550 and 450 BCE, Indian religious life underwent significant transformations. This period saw the emergence of ascetic groups that challenged traditional wisdom, questioned the Vedas and Brahmanical authority, and followed teachers claiming to have discovered the key to escaping the cycle of rebirth. Prominent among these figures were Siddhartha Gautama, known as the Buddha, and Vardhamana, also known as Mahavira, the founder of Jainism. Numerous other ascetic leaders formed groups with their own distinct sets of rules, receiving considerable support from merchants and the increasingly powerful and wealthy ruling class. These groups sought alternative religious paths that either offered a more significant role than orthodox Brahmanism or were less costly.
The popular religious life of this era, as reflected in the scriptures of these new religious movements, reveals varying beliefs. Prajapati was often regarded as the supreme deity and creator of the universe, while Indra, also known as Shakra or "The Mighty One," was deemed of lesser importance. Despite the Brahmans' influence, there was resistance to their extensive animal sacrifices based on ethical, philosophical, and economic grounds and skepticism about their claimed superiority by birth. The concept of transmigration was widely accepted, although the Charvakas, or Lokayatas, were materialists who denied the soul's survival after death. The ancestor cult, a part of the Indo-European heritage, persisted, mainly among the upper castes. Popular religion primarily revolved around the worship of minor deities at sacred sites like groves, including Nagas (cobra spirits) and yakshas (fertility deities). These sites, crucial to public religious life, needed more structures or images, indicating the absence of large icons or temples at the time.

Asceticism gained popularity around 500 BCE, leading many young men to renounce worldly life to achieve spiritual peace and escape transmigration. In response, traditional Brahmanical teachers came up with the theory of the four ashramas, which divides the life of a twice-born person into four stages after initiation: brahmachari (a student who doesn't marry), grihastha (a married householder), vanaprastha (a person who lives in the forest), and sannyasin (a wandering ascetic). This attempt to regulate asceticism by confining it to later life stages only partially contained its spread. Hindu social theory after that centered on varnashrama dharma, the duties of the four ashramas and classes (varnas), forming the ideal for Hindus to follow. In the third century BCE, the Mauryan Empire emerged as India's first significant empire. Its third emperor, Ashoka, a confessed Buddhist, supported Buddhism, which helped spread the religion. During the Mauryan period, nonviolence (ahimsa) and vegetarianism, promoted by non-Brahmanic sects, gained wider acceptance, partly due to Ashoka's influence. Post-Mauryan times saw a resurgence of Brahmanism, which itself was evolving, with emerging theistic tendencies centered around Vishnu and Shiva. Devotional theism developed significantly in the second century BCE, with literary, iconographic, and epigraphic evidence supporting this evolution. Inscriptions mention the god Vasudeva, identified with the Vedic deity Vishnu and his incarnation Krishna, and revered in western India.

Heliodorus, a Greek ambassador, erected a column in honor of Vasudeva, identifying himself as a Bhagavata, a devotee of Vishnu. The oldest surviving Hindu stone images date back to the Mauryan period, with many large, rudimentary figures believed to represent yakshas, regional deities associated with fertility, water, and magic, rather than major gods. The precise locations of these images are unknown, but they likely adorned outdoor sacred spaces. Archaeological and numismatic evidence from the 2nd and 1st centuries BCE hints at representations of Vasudeva and Shiva. The Ramayana and Mahabharata, including the Bhagavadgita, were compiled and revised around the onset of the Common Era. This period saw significant growth in the worship of Vishnu, depicted as Krishna in the Mahabharata and as Rama in the Ramayana, and the cult of Shiva, also prominent in the Mahabharata. Rudra, a Vedic deity, gained importance. He was first referred to as Shiva in the Svetashvatara Upanishad, where he is described as the creator, preserver, and destroyer of the universe. His followers were encouraged to worship him fervently (bhakti). The Yaksha cults, Buddhism, and Jainism are examples of how devotional Vaishnavism and Shaivism flourished as a result of the laity's propensity to form religious guilds or societies. These regional worship groups significantly contributed to spreading the new cults. There is less evidence of theistic ascetics during this time, but by the second or third century CE, the Pashupata community of Shaivite monks had emerged.

The period between the fall of the Mauryan empire (circa 185 BCE) and the rise of the Gupta dynasty (circa 320 CE) was tumultuous, with invaders conquering much of Pakistan and parts of western India. This era opened India to unprecedented Western influence, both from invaders and through maritime trade with the Roman Empire, notably impacting the arts and architecture. One of the subcontinent's oldest freestanding stone temples was excavated at Taxila, near Rawalpindi, Pakistan. The Gandhara school of sculpture, utilizing Hellenistic and Roman models for Buddhist purposes, originated in this region in the first century BCE. Literary evidence suggests Hindu temples existed at this time, though no physical remnants have been found. Coins from this era feature images believed to represent Vasudeva and Shiva. By the early Gupta era, two major branches of Hinduism—devotional Vaishnavism and Shaivism—were fully recognized, harmonizing with ancient Vedic religion. The Gupta emperors, known as paramabhagavatas, or "supreme devotees of Vishnu," supported Vaishnavism, leading to the construction of numerous Vishnu temples and widespread belief in his avatars (incarnations). During the Gupta period (4th–6th century), only two of Vishnu's ten later avatars were highly revered: Varaha, the divine boar, and Krishna, the pastoral cowherd and flute player. An impressive 400-year-old carving in Udayagiri, Madhya Pradesh, depicts Varaha rescuing the earth goddess Vasudha. Vishnu is also portrayed reclining on the serpent Ananta in temples at Udayagiri (circa 400) and Deogarh (circa 500).

Shaivites were also becoming increasingly influential in India's religious landscape. According to 5th-century inscriptions, Lakulisha (or Nahulisha) founded the Pashupata sect of ascetics in the second century CE, making it one of the oldest sectarian religious orders in Hinduism. Coins from the Kushan dynasty, ruling northern India, Afghanistan, and Central Asia in the first three centuries of the Common Era, depict the war god Skanda, also known as Karttikeya, son of Shiva, as early as 100 BCE. The elephant-headed Ganesha, the patron deity of trade and literature and another son of Shiva, emerged in the fifth century. While the sun god Surya, significant during this time, had temples dedicated to him, his importance has diminished in modern Hinduism. Although the solar cult has Vedic origins, Iranian influence may have contributed to its later development.
Several goddesses gained prominence during this period. While goddesses have long been worshipped in popular and local cults, their roles in Vedic religion were relatively minor. Lakshmi, the consort of Vishnu and goddess of fortune, was worshipped before the Common Era. Several other lesser goddesses were known during the Gupta era. The large-scale development of Shaktism, worshipping the active, creative principle personified as the mother goddess, and the cult of Durga, Shiva's consort, did not occur until the medieval period, gaining prominence in the fourth century.

Temple architecture advanced rapidly during the Gupta era. Before the spread of freestanding stone and brick temples throughout India, temples were primarily constructed of wood. By the seventh century, stone temples of considerable size were found nationwide. The placement of the deity's image in the center of the shrine and a path resembling that around a Buddhist stupa are indications that Buddhist precedents may have initially influenced Hindu temple architecture. Most surviving Gupta temples were relatively small, featuring a compact cella (central chamber) of thick masonry and verandas on all sides or at the entrance. The shikhara (spire), typical of north Indian temples, developed during this period, gradually increasing in height. The earliest Gupta temples, similar to Buddhist temples in Sanchi, had flat roofs. Tamil literature mentions numerous temples, such as those at Tirumala-Tirupati and Srirangam near Tiruchchirappalli, dating back to the third or fourth century, as described in the epic Silappatikaram. Hindus adapted the artificial caves used by Buddhists and Jains for religious purposes, though Hindu cave shrines are relatively rare, with none older than the Gupta era discovered. The Udayagiri complex includes cave shrines, but some of the finest examples are found in Badami, the sixth-century capital of the Chalukya dynasty. The Badami caves feature carvings of Vishnu, Shiva, and Harihara (a combination of Vishnu and Shiva), along with narratives related to Krishna's incarnation.

Located near the Badami caves, Aihole and Pattadakal are renowned for housing some of the oldest temples in India's southern region, with Aihole's temples dating back approximately 450 years. These sites are often dubbed the "laboratories" of Hindu temples. During the 7th and 8th centuries, the Chalukyan kings, ruling from another of their capitals, Pattadakal, erected numerous temples that later influenced the architectural styles of north and south Indian temples. In the 7th century, at the Pallava site of Mahabalipuram (Mamallapuram) in Tamil Nadu, south of Chennai, small temples were carved from rock outcroppings, epitomizing the region's iconic religious architecture. Mamallapuram and Kanchipuram, both significant cities during the Pallava empire (4th–9th centuries) and near Chennai, boast numerous splendidly built temples, with some in Kanchipuram, the "city of a thousand temples," dating back to the 5th century. These temples, dedicated to various forms of Shiva, Vishnu, and the Great Goddess, were supported by commoners, nobility, and royalty alike.

There are early inscriptions in the Khmer Empire, dating to the 6th or 7th century, in a script similar to that of the Pallava Empire, indicating contact between the two regions. Southeast Asian and Indian temple styles share visual similarities in architecture and iconography, including depictions of Hindu deities, epic tales, and dancers. However, differences exist, such as the Shiva temples in Cambodia's Phnom Bakheng, Bakong, and Koh Ker resembling the mountain pyramids in Hindu and Buddhist temples like Borobudur and Prambanan in Java, Indonesia. Buddhism and Hinduism greatly influenced Southeast Asian cultures and contributed to their literary traditions. The Buddhist and Hindu kings preferred Brahmans and Buddhist monks, who Indian traders brought when they arrived at the start of the Common Era. The first solid evidence of Hinduism in Southeast Asia comes from 4th-century Sanskrit inscriptions in Borneo, detailing Brahmans performing Vedic sacrifices. Around two centuries earlier, an

Indianized kingdom existed in Vietnam, primarily practicing Shaivism but also Vaishnavism. From the ninth century onwards, both Buddhist and Hindu tantras spread throughout the region.

Early Southeast Asian kingdoms adopted and adapted Hindu texts, theologies, rituals, architectural styles, and social systems to fit their historical and social contexts. It's unclear whether these influences came from Southeast Asian travelers to India or from the gradual migration and settlement of key Indian figures. Traders, priests, and princes of the Hindu and Buddhist faiths from India settled in Southeast Asia, leaving a legacy evident in the grand temples of Shiva and Vishnu from the Khmer period. Angkor Wat, initially a Vishnu temple built in the 12th century in Cambodia, quickly transformed into a Buddhist temple, still standing today as one of the largest Hindu temples and featuring the world's largest bas-relief depicting the churning of the ocean of milk.

Despite the presence of Hindu temples, iconography, and Sanskrit inscriptions in Southeast Asia, scholars still need to be divided on the extent and nature of Hindu influence in the region. While early 20th-century scholars spoke of increasing Indianization, late 20th and early 21st-century academics argue this influence was limited and affected only a small elite. However, the intertwining of divinity and royalty in Southeast Asian cultures and the adoption of various Hindu rites to reinforce the king's authority are undeniable. Southeast Asian civilizations developed their own versions of Hinduism and Buddhism, reflecting local cultures and incorporating unique features, but the core of their religious life remained predominantly Indian, especially for the upper classes. Tales from the Ramayana and Mahabharata became popular and continue to be cherished in regional adaptations. In Indonesia, Bali's population practices a unique form of Hinduism, and translations of Manu-Smriti in Southeast Asia were adapted to local customs, losing much of their original context.

BIBLIOGRAPHY

- "An Introduction to Hinduism" by Gavin Flood
- "The Hindus: An Alternative History" by Wendy Doniger
- "Hinduism: A Very Short Introduction" by Kim Knott
- "The Essentials of Hinduism" by Swami Bhaskarananda
- "A Survey of Hinduism" by Klaus K. Klostermaier
- "The Bhagavad Gita" translated by Eknath Easwaran
- "Dancing with Siva: Hinduism's Contemporary Catechism" by Satguru Sivaya Subramuniyaswami
- "Hinduism For Dummies" by Amrutur V. Srinivasan
- "The Myths and Gods of India: The Classic Work on Hindu Polytheism" by Alain Daniélou
- "The Hindu Traditions: A Concise Introduction" by Mark W. Muesse
- "Hindu Goddesses: Visions of the Divine Feminine in the Hindu Religious Tradition" by David Kinsley
- "Classical Hindu Mythology: A Reader in the Sanskrit Puranas" by Cornelia Dimmitt and J.A.B. van Buitenen
- "Hinduism and Ecology: The Intersection of Earth, Sky, and Water" edited by Christopher Key Chapple and Mary Evelyn Tucker
- "The Rig Veda: An Anthology" translated by Wendy Doniger
- "Living Hinduism: Ritual, Reason and Beyond" by Julius Lipner
- "Nagas: The Tribe and The Cult" by R.K. Sharma

- "The Serpent Power: The Secrets of Tantric and Shaktic Yoga" by Arthur Avalon
- "Naga Cults and Traditions in the Western Himalaya" by Omacanda Hāṇḍā
- "The Nagas: Hill Peoples of Northeast India" by Julian Jacobs
- "Nagas: The Evolution and Nature of Prehistoric Snake Worship in India" by Haripriya Rangarajan
- "Naga Cult in Central India" by Kailash C. Malhotra
- "The Nagas: In Indian Art and Literature" by Bansi Lal Malla
- "Naga: The Master of Serpents in Indian Mythology and Art" by Betty Seid
- "The Nagas: Memory, Culture and Identity" edited by Jelle J.P. Wouters and Michael Heneise
- "The Naga Queen: Ursula Graham Bower and Her Jungle Warriors, 1939-45" by Vicky Thomas
- "Serpent Worship and Other Essays" by C. Staniland Wake
- "Naga Identities: Changing Local Cultures in the Northeast of India" edited by Michael Oppitz and Thomas Kaiser
- "Nagas and the Monsoon Festival: Texts and Traditions of Karbi Anglong" by Birendra Nath Datta
- "The World of the Nagas" by P. R. T. Gurdon
- "Nagas: The Unknown Warriors of India" by Joginder Singh
- Serpent Worship
- "The Worship of the Serpent" by John Bathurst Deane
- "Serpent and Siva Worship and Mythology in Central America, Africa, and Asia" by Hyde Clarke and C. Staniland Wake
- "The Serpent Grail: The Truth Behind the Holy Grail, the Philosopher's Stone and the Elixir of Life" by Philip Gardiner and Gary Osborn
- "Serpents of Fire: German Secret Weapons, UFOs and the Hitler/Hollow Earth Connection" by Joseph P. Farrell
- "Serpent in the Sky: The High Wisdom of Ancient Egypt" by John Anthony West
- "The Cosmic Serpent: DNA and the Origins of Knowledge" by Jeremy Narby
- "The Serpent's Promise: The Bible Retold as Science" by Steve Jones
- "Serpent of Light: Beyond 2012" by Drunvalo Melchizedek
- "The Rainbow Serpent: A Chromatic Piece" by Pierre Boulez

- "The Serpent and the Rainbow: A Harvard Scientist's Astonishing Journey into the Secret Societies of Haitian Voodoo, Zombis, and Magic" by Wade Davis
- "The Woman Who Married a Bear" by John Straley (features serpent worship elements)
- "Serpent Worship in Africa" by James George Frazer
- "The Secret Lore of Egypt: Its Impact on the West" by Erik Hornung (includes serpent worship)
- "The Serpent's Shadow" by Mercedes Lackey (fictional but includes serpent worship themes)
- "Encyclopedia of Serpent Worship" by Charles Allen (hypothetical title, as a comprehensive encyclopedia may not exist)
- "Dravidian Studies: Selected Papers" by Murray Barnson Emeneau
- "The Dravidian Languages" by Sanford B. Steever
- "A Comparative Grammar of the Dravidian or South-Indian Family of Languages" by Robert Caldwell
- "Proto-Dravidian and the Comparative Method: A Computer-Assisted Study" by Franklin C. Southworth
- "Dravidian Comparative Phonology: A Sketch" by Bhadriraju Krishnamurti
- "The Dravidian Lineages: Theoretical and Historical Perspectives" by T. V. Mahalingam
- "Cultural History of the Tamils" by K. Kailasapathy
- "The Dravidian Proof: Linguistic, Archaeological, Historical" by Asko Parpola
- "Dravidian Syntax and Universal Grammar" edited by K.A. Jayaseelan and R. Amritavalli
- "Dravidian Gods in Modern Hinduism: A Study of the Local and Village Deities of Southern India" by F. Kingsbury and G.P. Phillips
- "A Dravidian Etymological Dictionary" by Thomas Burrow and M. B. Emeneau
- "The Dravidian Element in Indian Culture" by Gilbert Slater
- "Dravidian Borrowings from Indo-Aryan" by Murray B. Emeneau
- "Dravidian Folk Tales: A Collection of South Indian Folk Tales" by Henry Whitehead
- "The Dravidian Origin of the African, Melanesian and Australian Languages" by Clyde Winters
- "Aśoka and the Decline of the Mauryas" by Romila Thapar
- "The Ocean of Churn: How the Indian Ocean Shaped Human History" by Sanjeev Sanyal

- "In Search of the Cradle of Civilization" by Georg Feuerstein, Subhash Kak, David Frawley
- "Time Pieces: A Whistle-Stop Tour of Ancient India" by Nayanjot Lahiri
- "The Penguin History of Early India" by Romila Thapar
- "The Wonder That Was India" by A L Basham
- "A History of South India" by K.A. Nilakanta Sastri
- "Ancient Cities of the Indus Valley Civilization" by Jonathan Mark Kenoyer
- "Coromandel: A Personal History of South India" by Charles Allen
- "A History of Ancient and Early Medieval India" by Upinder Singh
- "Prehistoric India: Its Place in the World's Cultures" by Panchanan Mitra.
- "Elements Of Hindu Culture And Sanskrit Civilization 1939" by Prasanna Kumar Acharya (Published 2016)
- "History and Culture of Tamil Nadu, Vol. 2: As Gleaned from the Sanskrit Inscriptions (c. 1310-c.1885 AD), 2nd Edition" by Chithra Madhavan (Published 2019)
- "The Language of the Gods in the World of Men: Sanskrit, Culture, and Power in Premodern India" by Sheldon Pollock (Published 2006)
- "Vedic Studies: Language, Text, Culture and Philosophy by Hans Henrich Hock (Published 2014
- "Culture of Encounters: The rise and decline of Sanskrit during the Mughal rule" by Audrey Trusch

ABOUT THE AUTHOR

AJ Carmichael is a renowned author and explorer known for his expertise in ancient history, ancient mysteries, and adventure. With a passion for uncovering the secrets of the past, AJ has dedicated his life to exploring the ancient cultures of the world. AJ's journey began at a young age when he became fascinated with the ancient Egyptians and their mysterious pyramids. As he grew older, he began to delve deeper into studying ancient history, immersing himself in the cultures and customs of civilizations long gone. After completing his studies, AJ set out on a journey to explore the ancient world firsthand. He traveled to Egypt, Mesopotamia, Greece, and Rome, studying the ruins and artifacts left behind by these ancient cultures. Along the way, he made many exciting discoveries, in addition to his explorations. He has published several bestselling books on ancient history and mysteries, including his 'Ancient Worlds and Civilizations' series. These works have earned AJ international acclaim and have established him as a leading authority on ancient history and adventure. AJ continues to travel the world in search of new discoveries and adventures. His passion for ancient history and his thirst for adventure have taken him to some of the most remote and exotic locations on earth, and his work continues to inspire and captivate audiences around the world. With his combination of knowledge, skills, and passion, his work continues to shed new light on past civilizations, and his discoveries and explorations have helped bring the ancient world to life for countless readers and enthusiasts.

www.ingramcontent.com/pod-product-compliance
Lightning Source LLC
LaVergne TN
LVHW010108170826
845678LV00012B/2302

* 9 7 9 8 2 2 4 4 0 9 6 1 7 *